Plan Now,
Retire Happy

Also by Alvin Hall
Money for Life
Winning with Shares
Your Money or Your Life
You and Your Money
What Not to Spend

Plan Now, Retire Happy

How to secure your future, whatever the economic climate

Alvin Hall

HODDER &
STOUGHTON

First published in Great Britain in 2009 by Hodder & Stoughton
An Hachette UK company

1

A CIP catalogue record for this title is available from the British Library

ISBN 978 0340 833582

Typeset in Sabon MT by Palimpsest Book Production Limited,
Grangemouth, Stirlingshire

Printed and bound by Clays Ltd, St Ives plc

Hodder & Stoughton policy is to use papers that are natural, renewable and
recyclable products and made from wood grown in sustainable forests. The logging
and manufacturing processes are expected to conform to the environmental
regulations of the country of origin.

Hodder & Stoughton Ltd
338 Euston Road
London NW1 3BH

www.hodder.co.uk

To my friend Josephine, who knew what she wanted, was financially wise, and achieved her goal of retiring happily in her little cottage overlooking the sea.

Contents

Acknowledgements

I owe a special thank you to three people. Sarah Pennells, my friend and financial journalist, generously helped me maintain the accuracy and timeliness of the information in this book. She also offered insightful criticism that proved essential in helping me refine the best approach to communicating the information in various segments of this book. Malcolm Cuthbert, of Killik & Co, patiently and precisely aided me in unravelling the language and details of some of the more complex pension issues. His historic perspective and knowledge of details are impressive. And as always, my long-time collaborator and friend, Karl Weber ably assisted me in creating a good foundation upon which to build a useful and informative book.

Everyone at Hodder and Stoughton, Rowena Webb, Cecilia Moore, Emily Heyworth-Dunn, the design group and especially the publicity and marketing teams who have shown enormous patience over the time it took me to produce the final manuscript that was acceptable to all of us. And finally, thanks to my agent, Vicki McIvor, and everyone at Take3Management for their ongoing support, wise advice, and humour.

Introduction: Retirement Myths, Retirement Realities

'What are your retirement dreams?' This is the question I began asking friends and acquaintances of all ages when I started writing this book. The responses were wide-ranging, revealing, sometimes funny, but all said in a tone of voice that reflected the financial uncertainties created by the recession and the pervasive distrust that has become associated with pensions – both rightly and wrongly.

My friend John, in his late 20s, said, 'My dream is to retire at age 45, but maybe a little later now, and to be able to play golf whenever I want to.'

Paul, in his mid-30s, said, 'I'll leave the daily commute behind at some point, I don't know when, and spend my time growing wine grapes on a hillside in Tuscany.'

Anita, in her mid-40s, said, 'I'm dreaming about long vacations, warm weather and a yacht in the south of France. Maybe I'll just settle for a nice little cottage in a warm climate beside the water.'

Janet, in her early 50s, said, 'I'm never going to retire. I've banished the word from my vocabulary! And it's a good thing that I have, given what's happened to the value of my pension.'

Richard, another friend in his 50s, admitted with some reluctance that he had not saved enough money and could only dream of retirement, and that the current drop in the stock market and property prices had just made his situation worse. He is quietly and anxiously scrambling to come up with both a plan for a modest retirement and the money to fund it.

As for me, now that I've entered my age-denying years, my dream of retirement isn't about any specific life programme. Instead, it's about having the mental security of knowing I have enough money to let me relax when I want to and work when I want to. The key is that whether I work or play, the choice should be *mine*. That's what I call a dream come true!

'And how are you going to fund your dreams?' This was my follow-on question – the money question. Given the anxieties about the current economic crisis, the responses were, as I would have expected, more vague and less varied. Most people answered with, 'I'll figure it out before I get there,' or some variation on that statement. 'I guess I'll have to save more, if I can find the money' was another common response, often stated wistfully. And a few said, with a little resignation and bitterness, 'I may have to work until I can't.'

Surprisingly few people I spoke to had real, concrete ideas about how they would fund their retirements. Many had no retirement savings to speak of. Many were relying heavily on the future value of and income from property or properties they owned. And even those who participated in company pension plans or had personal pensions were vague about how their pensions were performing or how much money they might get on retirement – until the recent recession woke them up to the risk of placing their retirement on autopilot. Even now, many were more or less drifting towards some unknown result – partly because they didn't want to deal with the sharp decline of their net worth (property, investments, pensions) brought about by the recession, or because they didn't know what to do, much like a deer caught in the headlights of a speeding car.

Paula, in her 50s, was one of the few with an actual plan. 'My parents will fund my retirement,' she told me.

I found this a surprising notion, but I must admit not a totally uncommon one. 'How awfully generous of them!' I responded.

'Oh, they don't *know* about it,' Paula corrected me. 'But when they die, I'll inherit their savings and sell their house. That will be my retirement nest egg.' A realistic plan? Only time – and the unwinding of Paula's parents' estate – will tell.

Unfortunately, relying on a substantial inheritance isn't an option available to me, and it may not be for you, either. And as most people realise, your government pension will support only a very basic retirement lifestyle, not the stuff that dreams are made of. Like me, you will probably have to provide the majority of the money for your retirement through a combination of a company or private pension scheme, and private savings.

It's a serious responsibility, one that you may have only just begun to get your mind around. Certainly the current economic contraction has made all of us aware that we must pay attention to planning for our retirement if we want to make our dreams reality. I've written this book to help you with the process. Whether you are in your 20s, 30s, 40s, 50s or early 60s, and whether you are earning a little or a lot, single or married, working for a big company or self-employed, this book will tell you in plain, clear language what you must do in order to achieve your own retirement dreams, whatever they may be.

Don't expect miraculous solutions. I can't tell you the winning numbers in next week's lottery or the name of a stock that will rise in value by 1,000 per cent over the next five years. And even if I, or anyone else, had warned about the drop in share prices and property values, most people would not have listened. History shows that at some point in a period of long economic growth and upward price movement in property and securities, every generation comes to believe that they have entered a period of unlimited growth. This belief slowly evolves, at almost all economic levels, into a sense of entitlement. And people don't want to hear any voice that's counter to that forever rosy economic future.

What I can give you in a book about retirement are some time-tested strategies that have worked for others and can work for you. I'll help you understand your saving and investment options so that you can make appropriate choices for yourself, just as I and many people I know have done. Importantly, I'll also tell you the risks and pitfalls to watch out for before you implement a plan, while you're saving and investing, and after you retire and begin to use your accumulated wealth.

By picking this book off the shelf, you've taken an important first step to making your retirement dreams come true. But the next step is just as important and a bit more challenging: seeing through the six big myths that prevent most people from creating a sound financial plan for retirement. I've become very familiar with these myths in my work as a financial educator and guide on my television programmes about personal finance. If I had a pound for every time I've heard one of them on the lips of people just like you – well, let's just say that my own pension pot would be a lot bigger than it is!

Let's go through these six myths together. Which ones have been holding *you* back?

'Retirement talk? That's for the 50-and-over set!'
This is a natural assumption. For most people, retirement arrives in their mid-60s, and few of us are accustomed to planning for events that are more than ten years in the future. Sometimes it's all we can do to figure out what to have for dinner tonight!

Images in magazines and on television also promote this myth. They illustrate stories about retirement planning with images of vibrant-looking older people with silver hair and satisfied smiles. The implication: if you're still young, you can tune out the conversation until another couple of decades have passed.

People who accept this myth avoid thinking about retirement until it's staring them in the face – usually when they hit the half-century mark. Suddenly they realise that retirement is just a few years away. They find themselves scrambling to pull together a package of money on which they can live after retirement. For millions, it's too little and too late. The fact is that saving enough for a comfortable old age in the space of just ten or fifteen years is very difficult for most people to pull off. They simply don't have enough spare money to save after paying all their current bills.

This is why waiting until you're in your 50s is a big mistake . . . and an alarmingly common one. People who discover in their 50s or later that they haven't saved enough for retirement are usually forced to make hard, unpleasant choices they never imagined having to make.

The lesson: if possible, start planning for retirement while you're still young. Begin following the advice in this book in your 20s or 30s and you might even find yourself having easy and pleasant choices to make: 'Should I retire early? Would I prefer a house by the beach or a posh city apartment? Would it be more fun to cruise the Greek isles next year or go on an African safari?' Those are the kinds of problems I want every reader of this book to face!

'Save my money? I'm having too much fun spending it!'
This is how nearly every young person feels when they first start earning money. I certainly did! Back in my 20s, when I first entered the workforce, my salary was small, just a little more than I needed to cover the basics – my rent, food and repayments on university loans. I was keen to use the meagre sum I had left over for a few enjoyable treats – fashionable clothes,

concerts, theatre and dinners out with friends. Saving for retirement seemed like a boring chore whose importance I glimpsed only distantly, if at all.

But those who *do* start saving when they're young – even in a small way – are always happy they did. Take Peter, a young man I recently met. At age 19, he'd begun making money as a professional skateboarder. (That's one of those occupations we Baby Boomers find it hard to imagine – a career path we certainly never dreamed about when we were Peter's age.) It was not by any standard a lot of money, but enough that it sparked his desire to do one thing – spend. Like most young people, regardless of the amount of money they are earning, he viewed his income almost as play money or funding for the exciting pastimes he was discovering.

Luckily for Peter, he had a good relationship with his father, who was a wise and thoughtful man. He sat Peter down and talked him into opening a pension plan. At the time it seemed to Peter a 'sad' (Peter's word) thing to do with his money. But today he is in his early 30s and his thoughts have changed. Now working in radio, he sees how the money he began saving in his youth has grown. He realises that he has far more long-term security than if he'd spent every single pound he earned when he was 19. It's a comforting feeling that motivates him to continue contributing to his pension. And he's quietly pleased that he listened to his father's advice.

I hope you'll be inspired by Peter's story and see the possibilities in it as they relate to your life. Take the lesson from this story and start saving for retirement when you're young. You'll be glad you did, just as he is.

'Contribute to a retirement plan – on my salary?
You must be joking!'
It's understandable when a low-paid worker, at any age, makes this complaint. In the early years of your career, there's rarely

enough money to cover all the things you really need, let alone the many things you might want. But this myth ignores a basic truth: the earlier you start saving, the lower the cost of your retirement. And this is true even when the amount you save is small. *Time* is the key factor. Few forces are as powerful as compound interest with time on its side. For example, suppose you put aside £100 a month (that's less than £25 a week) starting at age 25. Your nest egg will grow to over £113,000 by age 60 (assuming a realistic 5 per cent average rate of return). Amazing, yes – but true. Now imagine how much more you'd have if you periodically increased the amount you contribute.

So start accumulating money – even small amounts – for your retirement early. When I look back on my life, my second greatest financial regret is that I didn't start saving soon enough. (My greatest? Not marrying somebody who is very wealthy, of course!)

And if you wonder where the money to begin saving will come from, just imagine the kind of fund you can build by drinking a few pints less each week, giving up smoking, buying fewer DVDs, going to the race track less often, or buying one less outfit every month. If you really put your mind to it, you'll be surprised to discover how many ways there are to set aside a couple of pounds here, a few pounds there. (And if you do cut back on drinking, smoking, gambling and other such habits, you may benefit in ways that go beyond the purely financial.)

But remember: the sooner you start, the better! Don't give in to the myth that a young person can't afford to save. It's just not so – as Peter and many others like him have shown.

'I'm no financial genius. Planning for retirement is too complicated for me!'
It's true that retirement planning can be complex. There are many options available for retirement saving and investment. There are employer-sponsored plans, including some that let you make additional contributions beyond the amounts your

employer provides. There are private plans. There are plans that let you put money away before taxes, after taxes, or both. Each type of plan has its advantages and disadvantages.

So feeling a little overwhelmed is understandable, but it's foolish to let this stop you from getting started. The solution is the same as when tackling any other complex topic: keep it simple. Start by saving an amount you can afford and putting it into an investment vehicle you can understand (I'll provide all the basic know-how you need in this book). Over time, as your financial circumstances change and your knowledge grows, you can modify your pension plan if you like, making it more sophisticated and powerful.

But don't wait until you're an expert – start now! And drop the myth that retirement planning is too difficult for someone like you. If you're smart enough to use a PC, programme a mobile phone, or download tunes to an MP3 player, I promise you're smart enough to launch and build an effective retirement plan for yourself.

'Can't someone take care of retirement planning for me – or at least tell me exactly what to do?'
The misplaced desire to rely on someone else to make your retirement planning decisions arises from two sources. First, there's the fear that you can't possibly master all the details of personal finance. But as I've already suggested, you don't need to be an expert to begin saving and investing. Start small, start simple and enjoy watching your self-confidence, your knowledge, and your money grow together.

Second, there's the exaggerated perception many people have about the power of experts. They rely on doctors to fix their physical ailments, car mechanics to repair their cars and electricians to mend the wiring in their houses. In just the same way, they reason, there should be experts available to manage their saving and investment needs. However, because most people have no idea about how or where to find a financial expert, this myth becomes yet another excuse for doing nothing.

As someone who makes a living by offering people my financial expertise, I know that such knowledge can be very valuable. But responsibility for your life begins and ends with you. You know better than to drive your car recklessly in bad weather. You know that eating junk, drinking to excess and smoking up a storm are good ways to die young. And you know that plugging too many appliances into a single electrical socket can overload the circuits and cause a fire. If you ignore these simple precautions, neither a car mechanic, a physician nor an electrician can do much to fix the damage you're likely to cause.

Well, a person who refuses to start saving and investing for retirement is being just as reckless – but with his or her financial future. And if you're in this category, there's little an investment expert can do to help you. The first move is up to you.

If you do use the services of a financial planner or adviser, don't expect to abdicate your decision-making role. Instead, think in terms of a partnership. The two of you should be working together for one goal: your well-funded retirement. Talk with your adviser about your goals, your fears and your tolerance for risk. Don't hesitate to ask questions, even foolish or apparently stupid ones. The more you do, the better you'll become at steering your own financial ship.

A little later in this book, I'll offer more detailed tips about how to find, choose and work with a financial expert. But the most important tip is to discard the myth that someone else can fix your financial future. It's your life and your money, and only you can decide what to do with both.

'Retirement? Frankly, I doubt I'll even be living that long!'
I've often heard this excuse uttered with an air of knowing cynicism, as if planning for a long future is the act of a naïve or

foolish person. Yet life has a way of tricking us. I've seen many a person who assumed they would never reach retirement age suddenly realise that time has passed, seemingly in the blink of an eye. Retirement, either voluntary or involuntary, is already looming. Now, with the opportunity to prepare in advance long vanished, they can do nothing but lament, as jazz musician Eubie Blake did, 'If I'd known I was going to live so long, I'd have taken better care of myself!'

As with the other myths, the underlying attitude here is natural and understandable. When we're young it's hard even to imagine being old, but with a little luck we all get there eventually. And as medical science continues to advance, most of us can look forward to a longer life than our parents and grandparents enjoyed – and that means more retirement years to fund.

So please – even if you find it difficult to believe that one day you'll be looking in the mirror at the face of a 60, 70 or 80-year-old, accept the fact that it almost surely *will* happen one day. The only question is: will it be the face of an oldster who feels anxious, insecure and deprived, or that of a retiree brimming with confidence, optimism and exciting plans for tomorrow? The choice is yours.

Above all, don't let myths like these and stories of real disappointments and fraudulent activities discourage you from planning for your retirement. We've all read or heard the bad news and felt a deep sense of betrayal as pensions failed to keep their promises to people who invested in and believed in them for years. Don't let the myths, fear-mongering, mistakes, disappointments, betrayal and outright fraud cause you to do nothing. If they do, you'll end up being a victim – both of your own inaction and of the problems in our national and private pension programmes that especially affect those without plans of their own.

Are you a retirement dreamer? I hope so! The ideas, information and recommendations in this book will show you how to transform your dreams into solid realities. The sooner you begin, the easier it'll be. So turn the page and let's get started.

1. A Life Beyond Work:
Your Retirement Dreams

The Changing Face of Retirement

Not so long ago, retirement was more of a hope than a reality for the average working person. Some people simply couldn't afford to stop working at any age. They would work until health problems forced them to reduce their hours or stop completely. Because of short life expectancies in many countries, including the developed world, those who could afford to stop working at age 65 had, on average, only seven or eight more years of life to look forward to. Retirement was little more than a brief stopover between a life of hard work and, perhaps, a few years in a nursing home before the final 'retirement' to one's ultimate reward.

But in the last generation, all of this has changed. Thanks to improved medical care, nutrition, fitness and safety programmes, people in the developed world are living longer than ever. According to the UK Office for National Statistics, a man who retires in the year 2015 at age 65 can expect to live an additional 18 years, while a woman in the same circumstances will average 22 more years of life. And these are just average figures. A sizeable proportion of the population will live even longer, and higher percentages of people are surviving into their 80s and 90s than ever before. Similar patterns are turning up in the United States and in other advanced countries.

These changes mean that retirement planning needs to be a much different exercise for our generation than it was for our parents or their parents. Rather than assuming that we'll live after retirement for just a few years in a relatively sedentary way, we should assume two decades or more of retired life, much of it active and filled with new experiences.

Of course, this is wonderful news, but it also creates real challenges. How will you be able to afford the vibrant retirement lifestyle that modern medicine is making possible? How can you save and invest enough money during your income-earning years to tide you over through not seven or eight, but 20, 30 or even more non-earning years? And how will you be able to afford the many exciting opportunities that today's longer-lived, robust seniors can enjoy – travel, volunteerism, lifelong learning, and a host of other cultural, social and personal pursuits?

It's a nice problem to have, but it's a problem nonetheless, one that everyone must solve in a unique way, suited to their own resources, abilities, interests and needs.

Planning Your Retirement Lifestyle

Devising your personal solution to the retirement puzzle begins with some realistic thinking about what your life will be like after retirement. Where will you live? How will you spend your time? What will you need money for? These and many other questions must be answered – at least tentatively – before you can begin to develop a plan for making possible the retirement lifestyle you want.

One of the most basic issues you'll face is: will you retire at all – in the sense of leaving work completely behind? For growing numbers of people, the answer is No.

In 2005, the financial firm Merrill Lynch sponsored a survey of Baby Boomers, members of the enormous (and enormously influential) generation of people born between 1943 and 1964.

As I write, the older members of this generation are on the verge of retirement, the first of tens of millions of Boomers who will soon be redefining old age as well as straining the financial resources of government and corporate pension programmes the world over. It's noteworthy, however, that in the Merrill Lynch survey, fully 76 per cent of the Boomers studied said they hoped to continue working after retirement. Similar surveys in the UK have yielded comparable results.

The respondents to surveys like these aren't driven only by financial concerns. Many say they want to work well into their 60s because they enjoy the camaraderie, challenges and accomplishments they associate with work, not just the pay cheque.

This is a significant change from the attitudes of previous generations, many of whom are currently enjoying well-earned lives of leisure following decades of hard work (including raising their Baby Boomer children). Almost as soon as long-term retirement became a reality for millions of working people, the Boomers began to rethink it. (Not surprisingly, perhaps; ever since their youthful heyday in the 1960s, the Boomers have been notorious for their readiness to re-examine and challenge all kinds of social, economic and political arrangements.)

Many companies are now beginning to adjust to the changing expectations of their older workers. There are practical reasons for this shift. Many employers are eager to retain the wisdom and experience that their older employees have developed over the years. They worry that the relatively smaller size of the immediately succeeding generation – often known as Generation X – will make it impossible for them to replace the millions of workers who will be retiring in the decades to come with skilled managers and professionals in their 30s and 40s. Some human resource experts even speak about a 'talent crisis' as companies lose their Boomers and turn to Xers for leadership.

In response, companies are developing flexible work plans and 'flexible retirement' programmes that allow older employees to cut back on their hours while remaining on salary. For example, BT Group (formerly British Telecommunications) eliminated its traditional retirement age in 2006, allowing employees a free choice as to whether and how to remain employed in their 60s. To make good use of this new pool of seasoned talent, the company has created specially-designed programmes, such as a helpdesk staffed by workers aged 60 and over which caters specifically to older customers who are having trouble with high-tech services such as broadband connectivity. At Yorkshire Water, retirement-age employees are permitted to work part-time, draw part of their pension payments and even continue to contribute to their company pension plan for later use. This new flexibility represents a win-win evolution that will benefit both the workers and the companies they serve.

Some older people who want to go on working choose to do so in fresh settings. There are almost as many options as there are retirees with talent, energy and ideas. Some start their own companies, which may compete with, complement, or serve their former employers or occupy an entirely different business niche. Some become consultants, outside contractors or freelancers, offering their expertise on a for-hire basis to companies willing to pay for it. And some become paid trainers, teachers, coaches or mentors to new generations of professionals in their field, passing along their wisdom to those who can benefit from it.

On the other hand, for some people the idea of continuing to work after 65 isn't a realistic option. Their work may be physically taxing, they may suffer from physical ailments that make work overly stressful or they may work in occupations where a strict retirement age policy is enforced. Others work in industries where employment is stagnant or in decline, and where companies may be happy to be relieved of the relatively higher pay cheques drawn by their retiring workers. And still others may work in fast-changing fields such as high technology, and may be unable or unwilling to keep retraining themselves to stay up-to-date with the latest trends.

Of course, for many people, working past age 65 sounds like a horrendous idea. They can't wait to leave the office or the workshop behind and begin living a life of leisure.

Whichever camp you fall into, you need to begin thinking about these choices *now*, before retirement looms, so that the financial plans you develop can match the reality of your post-65 life. And once you've decided whether and how you will want to go on working after retirement, there are many more decisions to be considered, from matters of geography (where will you live?) to personal relationships (with whom will you spend most of your time in retirement?). All will have a bearing on the kinds of plans you make and the financial resources you'll need.

Exploring the Future of Your Dreams

To help you start developing a realistic retirement plan that fits your personality, your needs and your resources, I've developed the Retirement Lifestyle Quiz. It's designed to help you think about your retirement options, including some you have probably never thought of before.

I urge you to devote a couple of hours to taking the quiz now, before you tackle the later chapters in this book. This applies to you no matter what your age or present circumstances. If you're young, in your 20s or 30s, you may feel that some of the questions are hard to answer or even irrelevant since I'll be asking you to think about things you won't be doing for another 20 to 40 years. That's all right. Respond as best you can, devising answers that seem plausible to you now based on what you know about your personality, likes and dislikes, talents and interests. It's very likely that your answers will change in the future, along with your retirement plans. No problem – the important thing is to begin developing some plans now, so that as your preferences evolve, your retirement plans can keep pace.

Forcing yourself to begin thinking about possible retirement pathways now can have some surprisingly positive effects. Imagining a life after work can be a great way to discover some of your deepest interests, values and desires. Give yourself permission to fantasise: what would you do with your time and talent if you were freed from the requirement to work every day? Dreaming about that is the first step to making it come true. There are no guarantees, of course; but if you *never* give yourself permission to dream those dreams, you can be certain they will never come to pass.

And don't worry that fantasising about a life without work will somehow weaken your commitment to the daily job you currently hold. If anything, the opposite is more likely. Having a retirement dream in mind – one that's as vivid and appealing as possible – can be a wonderful motivator for hard work in the here and now. Isn't it nice to think that every day spent working – and every small sum you deposit from your pay cheque into your retirement savings account – can be a step on the path to an exciting, fulfilling future life?

If you're married or in some other kind of committed relationship, take the quiz with your partner. If you're not accustomed to sharing such planning with your spouse, now is a great time to begin to get used to it. Assuming you do retire together, you may be spending a lot more time with each other than you are accustomed to. Learning to communicate and make decisions together will be the key to enjoying your new-found freedom as a couple rather than wasting time and energy squabbling.

You'll probably find that you and your partner have different answers to some or all of the questions. That's natural and normal. It doesn't mean you can't create a mutually satisfying retirement lifestyle together; it just means that you need to devote time and energy to working out a compromise programme that includes as much as possible of what you each desire. Talk through all the areas of agreement and disagreement, and make certain that you really understand your partner's fundamental motivations and dreams. Don't just consider the surface of each question; delve into the underlying *whys*. Once you know *why* your partner dreams of living in a hut on a South Sea island, while you prefer to imagine life in a high-rise flat in a big city, you can work together on finding an alternative plan that can meet both sets of needs.

Write down your answers in a notebook so that you can reread, rethink and revise them later. Don't think of them as carved in stone. This is simply the very first pass at developing a plan for your future life – one that goes well beyond finances in its scope. You may find that some of the questions in this quiz touch on topics you've barely begun to think about. That's good! I'm hoping that this quiz – the first of many exercises you'll work through as you read this book – will be a first step on a journey of discovery.

The Retirement Lifestyle Quiz

1. Do you hope to quit your full-time employment one day? If so, when?

2. After you retire from your full-time employment, would you like to continue working in your current occupation on a part-time basis – for example, working fewer hours per week or only during selected seasons of the

year? Have you investigated whether or not this option is currently available in your field?

3. If part-time work in your current occupation figures in your retirement plan, what do you estimate as your monthly income from that source? Be conservative in making this calculation. (For every question in this quiz, use current money values without considering inflation.)

4. If you plan to leave your current occupation completely, are you considering developing a new career or starting a business of your own? If so, what might it be?

5. Have you investigated what it will take to launch this new career? Will you need educational credentials, licences, business connections, tools and equipment or other resources you don't currently have? If so, how long will it take to acquire them?

6. Will you need to make a financial investment to obtain the resources you need to change careers (for example, to pay for schooling or to purchase a business franchise)? If so, how much money will be required?

7. Do you dream about travelling after retirement? If so, where would you like to travel? List your preferred destination(s).

8. If travel is part of your retirement dreams, what form of travel do you fancy: first-class, with luxury accommodation; roughing it by camping out amid natural beauty; or something in between? Have you begun exploring the costs involved in your preferred form of

travel? If so, what would you consider a reasonable annual budget for travel during your retirement years?

9. Other than travel, what kinds of activities would you like to enjoy during your retirement years? Possibilities could include sports, hobbies, visiting family and friends, charitable or civic activities, arts and crafts, or education. List them.

10. Are the activities you've listed ones that you are already engaged in? If not, have you researched the costs and other requirements for participating? Are you certain that they will be enjoyable and rewarding for you?

11. After you retire, would you prefer to remain in your present home or to move?

12. If you plan to remain in your present home, when will the mortgage and any secondary secured loan be paid off? How much money will be freed up each month once you've paid off your mortgage?

13. If you are hoping to move after retirement, where would you like to live?

14. If you are considering moving to another town, district or country, how much time have you already spent visiting or living in that new location? How fully can you anticipate the realities of life in your new home, such as climate, shopping, access to health care, cultural opportunities and the social scene?

15. Have you investigated the availability of appropriate housing in the places you are considering moving to?

Can you accurately estimate the cost of a house or flat in your new location? Can you realistically estimate the difference between the amount you are now spending on housing and the amount you will spend after retirement?

16. Have you begun exploring other expenses involved in a possible move, such as daily living expenses, taxes, health care, the cost of travel (to visit family and friends) and so on?

17. What is your current health status? Do you have any chronic health conditions that limit your activity or require regular medical attention? If so, how might these conditions affect your future lifestyle plans?

18. Do you want to make one-off or regular gifts or financial contributions to your children, grandchildren or other relatives after retirement? If so, what amounts might be involved?

19. Does charitable giving to your church or other organisations play a significant role in your life? If so, what are the annual amounts you would like to be able to give?

20. Are there any other activities, experiences or lifestyle changes you've dreamed of that haven't yet been recorded or described in your answers to the previous questions? If so, capture them now.

Obviously, there are no right or wrong answers to this quiz, and no two people will answer the questions the same way – not even two people in the same household. The purpose of the quiz is not to produce a definitive retirement plan, but rather to sketch some of the most important retirement dreams you'd like to fulfil if you can. In the chapters that follow, we'll examine those dreams in much more detail, and look at what you need to do to make them achievable.

2. Putting a Price Tag on Your Dreams

What Will Your Retirement Cost?

Now that you've developed a first sketch of your retirement dreams, it's time to begin figuring out what kind of financial resources you'll need to make those dreams possible. Only then can you develop a savings and investment plan that will get you there.

The first step is to calculate the amount of income you'll need after retirement in order to afford the lifestyle you desire. That's the main purpose of this chapter. One very simple way to approach this challenge is to assume that you'll need about 75 per cent of your pre-retirement income to live comfortably after retirement. For example, suppose you retire at age 65 from a job where your final salary was £55,000 per year. According to this approach, your desired retirement income would be:

£55,000 x .75 = £41,250

This '75 per cent rule' is based on the notion that most retirees can reduce their living costs once they stop working. Expenses such as daily commuting, work clothes and lunches while at work can be eliminated. Furthermore, for many people, retirement age also corresponds to the time when other major life expenses tend to decline. For example, in many families, children graduate from university or college, move away from home and become financially independent when their parents are in their 50s or early 60s. And for some homeowners, mortgages get fully paid off around the same time.

The 75 per cent rule is a common assumption that many financial planners use. But like most assumptions, it may or may not stand up under closer scrutiny. For one thing, it assumes that your pre-retirement income is enough to support a 'comfortable' lifestyle, however you define it. If you are just barely scraping by while working full-time, it's very possible that 75 per cent of your present income will be little more than adequate.

Furthermore, it may or may not be true that your other expenses, such as child-rearing and home mortgage costs, will go down around the time you retire. Some people have children who need ongoing support well into their adult lives, including children with physical or psychological disabilities. And some people purchase homes in their 40s, 50s or later, and carry mortgages that will not be fully paid off until their 70s or beyond.

So the 75 per cent rule is not terribly reliable. For some people, 75 per cent of their pre-retirement income will accommodate a very comfortable life. For others, it will be inadequate. Some retirees even find they spend *more* money after retirement than they did before, especially if travel, gifts to children and grandchildren, or expensive new hobbies and activities are part of their retirement lifestyle. And, of course, for some people, health care expenses in old age can become a significant cost.

Rather than rely on the 75 per cent rule, I recommend you invest a little more time in planning what you'll need to enjoy the kind of life you want to have in retirement. The Retirement Expense Planner is a more detailed and exact way of calculating what kind of income you'll need to enjoy a happy retirement lifestyle. It will take you an hour or two to complete, but the security and clarity of mind it will bring you will make it well worth the effort.

The Retirement Expense Planner

There are two stages to filling out this form (over the page). First, in Column A, you'll calculate how much you are *currently* spending (before retirement) in various categories of life expenses. Then in Column B, you'll estimate how these expenses are likely to change after you retire.

To fill in Column A, you can simply make your best guess as to the amount you spend per month on each type of expense listed. However, this is likely to produce figures that are vague and inaccurate (and probably too low). Instead, I recommend using at least six months' worth of bank statements and credit card bills to come up with accurate figures. For example, rather than guessing how much you spend on clothing, look through six months of statements and credit card bills, total the amount you spent on clothing during that time, and divide the result by six to yield a monthly amount.

For expenses that are highly irregular or seasonal, calculate an annual sum and divide it by twelve. For example, if most of your annual gift-giving is concentrated around Christmastime, figure out how much you spent last year, divide that amount by twelve, and put the result in Column A under 'Christmas/ seasonal gifts'. Similarly, if your home gas bill increases during the winter months because of the cost of home heating, add up a year's worth of gas bills, divide it by twelve, and use the resulting amount as the monthly figure for Column A.

Because of the irregularity of certain expenses, your Column A figures will be an average that is probably lower than your actual expenses in certain months, higher than in others, but on average about right.

To fill in Column B, try to estimate how the same expenses will change in retirement. Some categories of expenses may not change at all. For example, if you are planning to remain in the same home, at least at first, and if your mortgage will not be paid up for some time, your home expenses may be the same in Column B as in Column A. Other expenses may decline: for instance, if you no longer have to travel to work in an office, you may reduce your expenses for transport, dry cleaning and other work-related expenditures. However, other expenses may increase after you retire: with more time on your hands, you may spend more money on travel and entertainment than you do now. And because you will be at home more, the cost of heating, electricity and other utilities are likely to increase.

Try hard to make the figures in Column B as realistic as possible. A certain amount of guesswork is unavoidable, but when in doubt, err on the side of conservatism – that is, guess a bit *high* rather than a bit low. We all know that expenses have a way of creeping up rather than down, don't we?

When you've filled in all the relevant amounts, add the numbers to get the totals for each of the two columns.

Retirement Expense Planner

HOME:	Column A Current Monthly Spending (£)	Column B After Retirement Monthly Spending (£)
Mortgage or rent		
Electricity		
Gas		
Water rates		
Council tax		
Service charge		
Buildings insurance		
Contents insurance		
Other home (specify):		

TRANSPORT:	Current Monthly Spending (£)	After Retirement Monthly Spending (£)
Public transport		
Car loan repayment		
Car insurance		
Petrol/Diesel		
Road tax		
Taxis		
Other transport (specify):		

OTHER MONTHLY BILLS:		
Telephone (fixed line)		
Telephone (mobile)		
Child care		
Life assurance		
Income protection insurance		
Private health insurance		
Maintenance or child support		
Pension		
Endowments		
Other monthly bills (specify):		

DAILY LIVING:		
Food (at home)		
Lunch (at work)		
Cleaning supplies		
Health and beauty aids		
Laundry and dry cleaning		
Medicines and medical care		
Other daily living (specify):		

ENTERTAINMENT:		
Meals in restaurants		
Takeaways		

...cont	Current Monthly Spending (£)	After Retirement Monthly Spending (£)
Pub/off-licence/wine bar		
Tobacco		
TV licence		
TV digital channels fee		
Internet service		
Computer/electronic games		
Books, magazines, newspapers		
CDs, music		
Tickets for cinema, concerts, sports		
Sports/hobbies		
Club memberships		
Kids' activities		
Gambling/lotteries		
Home decoration		
Gardening		
Antiques/collectibles		
Other entertainment (specify):		

IRREGULAR EXPENSES:

	Current Monthly Spending (£)	After Retirement Monthly Spending (£)
Home repairs		
Appliances		
Car repairs		
Pets, including vet bills		
Holidays/travel		
Christmas/seasonal gifts		
Birthday and other gifts		
Clothing		
Toys (for children)		
School fees		
Hairdresser/barber		
Other beauty treatments		
Other irregular expenses (specify):		

DEBT REPAYMENTS (list them):	Current Monthly Spending (£)	After Retirement Monthly Spending (£)
MISCELLANEOUS CASH:		
TOTAL MONTHLY SPENDING:		

Once you've filled out the Retirement Expense Planner, you've taken the first big step towards developing a realistic idea of how much income you will need to enjoy the kind of retirement lifestyle you are planning. Congratulations! Many people never even get this far in the retirement planning process.

But we're not quite done with you yet. There are a couple of important factors you need to consider. (Don't worry, the remaining steps in this chapter will be a lot quicker and easier than the work you've done so far.)

The Effect of Income Tax

Although pensioners have higher allowances before their income is taxed than those under retirement age, they still have to pay income tax. This means that you'll need some extra money in your pocket in order to afford the kind of lifestyle you've outlined above.

Calculating the amount of tax you'll have to pay can't be done precisely. The tax rates, the amount of the personal allowance (that is, income on which no tax is due), and the taxable bands (that is, the income levels at which the tax rate increases) are all subject to change with each government budget.

However, the following figures will give you a general idea of what to expect.

For the tax year 2009–2010 (from 6 April 2009 to 5 April 2010), the personal allowances (income on which no tax is due) are as follows:

- For people below age 65: £6,475
- For people aged 65–74: £9,490
- For people aged 75 and over: £9,640

For the same tax year, the tax rates and taxable bands are:

- Starting rate (10 per cent) which only applies to income from savings: £0–£2,440
- Basic rate (20 per cent): £2,441–£37,400
- Higher rate (40 per cent): over £37,400

This means that your taxable income (that is, your income *above* the tax allowance) up to £2,440 is taxed at the 10 per cent rate if it arises from savings. (However, if you receive money from earned income or your pension, it is taxed at 20 per cent); your taxable income between £2,441 and £37,400 is taxed at 20 per cent; and your taxable income above £37,400 is taxed at 40 per cent.

Now, as I've said, these exact figures are apt to change slightly from year to year. And at this point, we haven't calculated your likely income after retirement – only how much your monthly expenses after retirement are likely to be. Nonetheless, based on the monthly expense figure you calculated using the Retirement Expense Planner, here's my rough rule of thumb for how much extra you need to allow for tax:

- Below £500 per month: 0
- From £583 – £1,000 a month: 10 per cent extra

- From £1,000 – £3,000 a month: 20 per cent extra
- From £3,000 – £7,000 a month: 30 per cent extra
- Over £7,000 a month: 40 per cent extra

Importantly, if the income comes from an ISA then there is no income tax to pay.

Take the Total Monthly Spending figure from Column B of the Retirement Expense Planner, multiply it by the appropriate tax percentage in the list above and add that amount to your Total Monthly Spending. This will give you a new (probably larger) sum, which is your monthly retirement spending *including* taxes.

For example, suppose your Total Monthly Spending from the Retirement Expense Planner came to £3,210 a month, since that figure falls into the 30 per cent range according to my tax rule of thumb, you need to add 30 per cent to your monthly retirement spending:

£3,210 x .30 = £963
£3,210 + £963 = £4,173

So your monthly retirement spending, including taxes, will be £4,173.

Still with me? Fine. Just one more step!

The Effect of Inflation

The role of inflation is another consideration that many people overlook. As you know, prices of goods and services have a tendency to rise over time. This means that a product that costs X amount today will probably cost at least a little bit more next year, and a little more the year after that, and the year after that, and so on. This phenomenon is known as *inflation*.

If you're a Baby Boomer like me, you remember the incredible and painful late 1970s and early 1980s, when inflation in the UK was between 8 per cent and 24.2 per cent. As a result, an item that cost £100 in 1974 would have cost double or triple just seven years later, in 1981. Not many people had salaries that could keep up with price increases like that; thus the purchasing power of every pound earned fell sharply!

Unfortunately, we are again in a period – beginning in 2008 – when the world economy is on a less stable footing. However, since 1993, the inflation rate has hovered around 2 per cent a year; though in late 2008 the Retail Price Index (RPI) reached 4.7 per cent. When undertaking short-term financial planning in such a historically low-inflation economic environment, the effect of inflation is so small and gradual that you can usually ignore it. (If you're saving for a holiday in the UK next summer, you don't need to worry about the few pounds by which a hotel stay may increase between now and then.) However, the current economic crisis, in which inflation has increased due to the prices of food, fuel and other commodities, illustrates why inflation must always be a factor in retirement planning. Over the long-term, even a relatively modest rate of inflation can have a significant effect on prices – and for most people, retirement planning is the longest term of all.

This means that inflation needs to be factored in when figuring out how much your retirement expenses will be. Let's say you've worked out that you will need £2,000 a month to live on in your retirement. Let's also assume that, in the next couple of decades, inflation will continue at approximately 3 per cent. In ten years' time, £2,000 will only buy the equivalent of about £1,475 in today's money. And in 20 years, the same £2,000 will only have the purchasing power of £1,088. You can see why: with prices rising by 3 per cent a year, the cup of tea that costs £1 today will cost £1.34 in ten years and £1.81 in 20 years, while all other goods increase at roughly the same rate (some more, some less).

To calculate how inflation may affect your retirement expenses, have a look at the Inflation Factor Calculator on page 36. In the left-hand column find the number of years that matches up with your expected retirement date. Then pick one of the five following columns, each representing a different inflation rate, from a low of 2 per cent to a high of 10 per cent. The box where the appropriate row and column meet contains your *inflation multiplier* – the factor by which expenses will increase over the time period and the inflation rate indicated.

For example, suppose you plan to retire in 20 years. If you think inflation during this period of time will average 4 per cent, look in that column and you'll find an inflation multiplier of 2.19. That means you should multiply your estimated monthly retirement expenses (including taxes) by 2.19. So if you think you'll be spending £2,700 a month, you will multiply:

£2,700 x 2.19 = £5,913

This means you will actually need £5,913 in 20 years in order to buy everything that £2,700 buys today.

Undoubtedly you are wondering which of the five inflation rate columns to go by – the very low 2 per cent, the somewhat alarming 10 per cent or something in between? Unfortunately, I can't tell you what the inflation rate will be between now and your retirement. (My time machine is down for repairs and my crystal ball turned cloudy years ago). This is one instance where your guess is literally as good as mine.

Many financial industry models currently in use assume 4 per cent inflation for the foreseeable future, so I suggest you use that figure. It's as good as any, and a trifle on the conservative side (since inflation has in fact been running below this rate over the past decade and a half).

Later in this book, I'll explain how you should monitor and update your retirement plan periodically. As part of that process, you will be redoing the inflation factor calculation once every six months (it's a simple calculation and won't take much time). If inflation were to significantly rise above 4 per cent (as it is measured by government price analyses and widely reported in the news), you can adjust your expense projections and make corresponding changes in your savings and investment plan. If it remains below 4 per cent, you can simply stay the course – the result will be a little extra cash in your account at the end of the day.

Inflation Factor Calculator

	Assumed inflation rate				
Years to retirement	2%	4%	6%	8%	10%
1	1.02	1.04	1.06	1.08	1.10
2	1.04	1.08	1.12	1.17	1.21
3	1.06	1.12	1.19	1.26	1.33
4	1.08	1.17	1.26	1.36	1.46
5	1.10	1.22	1.34	1.47	1.61
6	1.13	1.27	1.42	1.59	1.77
7	1.15	1.32	1.50	1.71	1.95
8	1.17	1.37	1.59	1.85	2.14
9	1.20	1.42	1.69	2.00	2.36
10	1.22	1.48	1.79	2.16	2.59
11	1.24	1.54	1.90	2.33	2.85
12	1.27	1.60	2.01	2.52	3.14
13	1.29	1.67	2.13	2.72	3.45
14	1.32	1.73	2.26	2.94	3.80
15	1.35	1.80	2.40	3.17	4.18
16	1.37	1.87	2.54	3.43	4.59
17	1.40	1.95	2.69	3.70	5.05

18	1.43	2.03	2.85	4.00	5.56
19	1.46	2.11	3.03	4.32	6.12
20	1.49	2.19	3.21	4.66	6.73
21	1.52	2.28	3.40	5.03	7.40
22	1.55	2.37	3.60	5.44	8.14
23	1.58	2.46	3.82	5.87	8.95
24	1.61	2.56	4.05	6.34	9.85
25	1.64	2.67	4.29	6.85	10.83
26	1.67	2.77	4.55	7.40	11.92
27	1.71	2.88	4.82	7.99	13.11
28	1.74	3.00	5.11	8.63	14.42
29	1.78	3.12	5.42	9.32	15.86
30	1.81	3.24	5.74	10.06	17.45
31	1.85	3.37	6.09	10.87	19.19
32	1.88	3.51	6.45	11.74	21.11
33	1.92	3.65	6.84	12.68	23.23
34	1.96	3.79	7.25	13.69	25.55
35	2.00	3.95	7.69	14.79	28.10
36	2.04	4.10	8.15	15.97	30.91
37	2.08	4.27	8.64	17.25	34.00
38	2.12	4.44	9.15	18.63	37.40
39	2.16	4.62	9.70	20.12	41.14
40	2.21	4.80	10.29	21.72	45.26

Once you've taken your estimated monthly retirement expenses (including taxes) and multiplied that figure by the appropriate inflation multiplier, you have a final monthly figure – your tax-and-inflation-adjusted monthly retirement expenses. Write that amount here:

£_____

This is an important number! It is the price tag for your retirement dream – and the target towards which all your retirement planning – including the savings and investment programme I'll be helping you develop in the later chapters of this book – should be aimed.

Of course, you'll want to remember that it is also a *moving* target, one that is subject to change as life circumstances dictate. Many factors might cause you to adjust your monthly retirement expenses figure. For example:

- With the kids grown up and out of the house, you decide to sell your large home and move to a smaller, less expensive place. *Reduce your monthly expenses.*
- You unexpectedly fall in love – with someone who has expensive tastes in holidays, clothes and jewellery. *Increase your monthly expenses.*
- After you retire, you discover that you and your partner can get along happily with just one car, since neither of you has to commute to work any longer. *Reduce your monthly expenses.*
- Your sister's marriage breaks up and she moves in with you 'just for a few weeks'. Weeks turn into months, then years. *Increase your monthly expenses.*

With a bit of imagination, you can think of many more possibilities. The point is that your retirement target must be constantly re-examined and adjusted as necessary, to keep up with your changing circumstances, needs and desires. By the end of this book, we'll have helped you set up an easy system for doing this on a regular basis.

Now you're ready for the next step in the process – figuring out how you might be able to pay the retirement price tag you've calculated. We'll tackle that challenge in the next chapter.

3. From Dreams to Reality:
Paths to Your Retirement Goal

Now that you've figured out how much money you need every month for a comfortable retirement, it's time to begin figuring out where the money will come from.

Fair warning: here is where the thickets grow a little dense. Over the years, a rather complicated set of programmes has grown up. They are designed to help older people meet their financial needs, but understanding how these programmes work, how they relate to one another and how you can make the most of what they offer can be a bit challenging. I'll walk you through the complexities one step at a time. By the time you finish this chapter, you should have a pretty good handle on how the system operates and where you fit in.

The Three-Legged Retirement Stool

If you've ever read anything about retirement planning, or even heard a report on radio or television about the topic, you may have encountered the image of the 'three-legged stool' as a way of thinking about retirement savings. It's such a familiar image that one might even call it a cliché. It's one of those clichés that has become popular for a very good reason: it's a clear and simple way of thinking about what you need to do to prepare for a comfortable and happy retirement.

A stool, after all, is about the simplest piece of furniture one can imagine. But there is one unique quality about a stool: it absolutely *must* have three legs to stand on. Any fewer and it is sure to tip over, leaving you embarrassed and perhaps injured on the floor. (Of course, a stool could have *more* than three legs, but three is the absolute minimum.)

In much the same way, smart thinking about retirement begins with three forms of financial support – the three legs of your stool. These three sources of income are each independent. This offers you financial security and risk reduction, since it's unlikely that all three or even two of the three will go belly-up simultaneously. And since you have some degree of control or at least influence over all three, especially early in life, you can make sure that your future is secure by working to make all three legs solid and dependable.

The three legs of a secure retirement are:

- **Your government pension.** If you've been working for a living – and in some cases, even if you have not – you are probably entitled to a State Pension, which will give you a small but secure source of income for as long as you live. Because it is government-funded, your State Pension is as solid and reliable as Her Majesty's government – which is to say, about as solid and reliable as anything can possibly be in the insecure times we live in. There are rumours that the government pension will come to an end. This is highly unlikely. What is more likely is that the pension will change as the country's demographics shift and the government's policies seek to respond to different economic needs. So don't expect them to stay the same.
- **Your employer or company pension.** This leg has often been called an occupational pension. In fact, the options in this area available to workers today are much broader. Many workers won't be able to participate in a traditional occupational pension, which could be a final salary or defined benefit scheme, or a money-purchase occupational

scheme. Instead, they will be able to join a group personal pension (GPP) or a stakeholder pension provided by their employer. While the participants may think of this as a 'works' or 'company' pension, if it is indeed a GPP or stakeholder, the employer does not have to contribute. Nonetheless, many company pensions are organised by and normally partly paid for by your employer. Exactly what you can expect from an employer or company pension is very variable, depending on the companies you've worked for, your income, the length of time you've worked, and the competence and integrity with which the pension scheme has been managed. For many people, this leg will provide a very solid, even generous basis on which to plan a comfortable retirement. For some, it may offer much less. Later, I'll tell you how to figure out where you sit and what to do about it.

- **Your personal savings and investment plan.** This third leg of the stool is completely up to you. Some misguided individuals, assuming that retirement is something 'someone else' will take care of, do little or nothing to create their own personal pension scheme. They are wholly dependent on the other two legs of their stool, and they may well be doomed to spending their final years teetering on the brink of disaster. Because you are reading this book, you are probably more foresighted than these people. By the time you finish reading, you'll have a good idea what you need to do to make sure that your third leg is as solid as the other two – perhaps more so – and feel confident that your retirement stool is strong enough to support you comfortably for life.

In later chapters, we'll delve in detail into how to make sure all three legs of your stool are secure. But in the next few pages, I'll give you an overview about each of the three legs so that you can put the many forthcoming details into a meaningful context.

The Role of Government

The pension paid by the British government is a complex business. There are lots of exceptions and sub-clauses in the rules that the government has established, and even if you get the full entitlement, the truth is that you will still be poor in retirement unless you have other sources of income. Nonetheless, the government pension is an important part of retirement planning for most people, and you owe it to yourself to invest a little time in figuring out what you are entitled to receive. The next few pages will get you started.

First, when are you entitled to receive payments? Currently, the age at which your State Pension payments will begin is set at 65 for men and at 60 for women. However, these ages will be changing.

Here is how women will be affected. Between 2010 and 2020, the State Pension age for women born after 5 April 1950 is due to rise. If you are a woman born on or before that date, your State Pension age will remain at 60. If you are a woman born between 6 April 1950 and 5 April 1955, your State Pension age will rise to between 60 and 65, depending on your exact date of birth. And if you are a woman born on or after 6 April 1955, your State Pension age will be 65.

Then, between 2024 and 2046, the State Pension age for both men and women is slated to increase from 65 to 68. You can find the exact date when you will reach State Pension age by visiting the following government webpage: http://www.thepensionservice.gov.uk/state-pension/age-calculator.asp.

Once you reach the eligibility date, you can retire from your job and begin receiving your State Pension. But you aren't *required* either to stop work or to begin receiving State Pension payments on your eligibility date. If you stop work but defer State Pension payments, you can increase the amount you'll begin receiving at a later date. Others choose to keep working beyond the eligibility date, while either receiving State Pension income or deferring it. We'll explain more about these options later.

The pension provided by the government consists of two parts – the basic State Pension and the additional State Pension. The full basic State Pension is currently (2009–10) set at £95.25 per week for a single person and £152.30 for a couple. State pensions are adjusted upwards every year in line with price inflation. However, they are falling year on year as a percentage of average earnings. Basically, what the state provides will probably be enough to keep you alive and with a roof over your head, but there won't be room for any luxuries.

To receive the full basic pension under the current rules, you must have paid contributions to National Insurance for nine-tenths of your working life – with certain exceptions we'll explain in a moment. For men, the working life is from age 16 to 65 = 49 years, so they must have paid contributions for 44 of these years. For women born before 1950 the retirement age is set at 60, but for those born after 1955 it is 65, and the number of years that contributions are required is set accordingly, varying between 39 and 44 years depending on their birth date.

Note, however, that the requirements are about to be significantly reduced. For people who will reach State Pension age after 6 April 2010, only 30 years of National Insurance payments will be required.

The great majority of working people – those earning more than £110 per week (as of 2009–10) from a single employer – pay National Insurance contributions through an automatic deduction from their wages. The amount you pay depends on how much you earn. You should be able to see how much you are paying by reviewing your pay slip. Your employer also makes a contribution on your behalf, and this figure should appear on your pay slip.

But if you don't fall into this category for your entire working life you may still qualify for the full basic State Pension, provided you fit into one of several groups of exceptions. The exceptions are as follows:

- If you earn between £95 and £110 per week (as of 2009–10) from a single employer, you will not pay National Insurance contributions, but you will be treated as if you have.
- If you have not made National Insurance contributions because you've been caring for small children, caring for someone who is sick or disabled, or too ill yourself to work, you may be granted National Insurance credits.

A self-employed person must make National Insurance contributions through direct payment to Her Majesty's Revenue & Customs – unless you've been granted permission *not* to make such contributions because of low earnings. Note that it's up to you to arrange such payments – the government will not come after you or claim the money automatically.

If you haven't paid enough contributions, you will get a portion of the full basic State Pension. The minimum pension payment is 25 per cent of the full pension (currently £23.81). This amount is paid to someone who has made qualified National Insurance contributions for 10 or 11 years (again, depending on his or her exact age).

If you're not sure how much National Insurance you've paid, you can apply for a forecast of your State Pension from the Department for Work and Pensions online at http://www.thepensionservice.gov.uk/resourcecentre/e-services/home.asp. You can also speak to a pensions adviser by telephoning 0845 300 0168.

If you find you haven't made enough qualifying contributions, you might be able to make up the deficit with some voluntary payments, and it could be well worth your while to do so.

So much for the basic State Pension. Now let's turn to the additional State Pension. The additional State Pension is also known as the State Second Pension (S2P). It was also previously known as the State Earnings-Related Pension Scheme (SERPS). If you were working and an employee between 1978 and April 2002, you will have been building your entitlement to SERPS. In this scheme, people with higher earnings built up more entitlement than low earners. Those who were self-employed or not earning at all did not build up SERPS entitlement.

Since April 2002, SERPS has been replaced by S2P, which is also linked to earnings during working life. The current maximum payment under S2P is £154.70 per week. The amount of S2P payment you'll receive after you reach pension age will rise with your pre-retirement income, up to a maximum income of £40,040 (as of 2009–10). However, S2P tops up those on lower incomes by offering a flat rate to those who earn between £4,940 and £13,900 a year (in which case you are treated as though you earn £13,900). Also, in most cases, those who care for the sick or disabled get automatic S2P credits.

At the moment, if you work for an employer and earn more than £4,940 annually, you will automatically be included in the S2P scheme unless you have *contracted out*. What does this mean? Here's the explanation.

Some company and personal pension schemes give you an option to have the relevant part of your National Insurance contributions paid in to them, instead of building up your entitlement for the additional State Pension. This is called contracting out. You might choose to do this if you believe you'll do better financially by investing with your employer's contracted-out pension scheme or your personal pension scheme as a Self Invested Personal Pension (SIPP) plan.

Not everyone should choose to contract out. It depends on your individual circumstances and the kind of financial return you expect to get from your contracted-out scheme. To help with this fairly complex decision, you may want to consult with an expert at The Pensions Advisory Service (TPAS), the independent state-run agency charged with providing such assistance. (Call them at 0845 601 2923.) Or you may want to discuss the issues with an independent financial adviser. I'll explain how to find and work with such an adviser in chapter 6.

If you do decide to contract out, you can change your mind at a later date. For example, if you change jobs, you might decide to participate in S2P under your new employer. Or you might simply decide, without changing jobs, that you aren't happy with the contracted-out scheme run by your employer or by your personal pension provider. Either way, you can begin contributing to your S2P scheme and building up your additional State Pension by contracting back in. Contracting out of the additional State Pension into a private pension is an option this government is planning to withdraw in 2012. From that date, S2P becomes a flat rate and you will not be able to opt out unless you are in an approved pension scheme provided by your employer.

If you're not sure about whether you've contracted out of S2P, you'll be told your current entitlement for S2P when you apply for your State Pension forecast. Or you can find out by calling the HM Revenue & Customs helpline at 0845 915 0150.

If your pension is very small and you don't have much saved, the government will top you up with a means-tested Pension Credit, or minimum income guarantee. This payment is currently set at £130 per week for a single person and £198.45 for a couple. You will get slightly more if you have your own savings (up to £10,000 from autumn 2009) and are aged 65 or over.

There are other forms of government aid available to people of retirement age. Other benefits you might be entitled to include travel cards; help with winter fuel bills, housing costs, council tax; bereavement allowance; and the costs of living with a disability. (Oh, and once you reach the age of 80, you'll receive an extra 25p per week on your State Pension. That will make all the difference, don't you think?)

Here are a couple of other important facts about the State Pension. First, although you are eligible to begin receiving State Pension payments once you reach your eligibility age, it will *not* happen automatically. It's up to you to make a claim. You will probably receive a form to use in claiming your payments around four months before your eligibility date. If you don't receive your form in the mail, you can download a copy from the Pension Service website.

Second, as we've already noted, you're not required to begin receiving State Pension payments once you reach the eligibility age. To defer payments, simply don't submit the claim form you received in the mail – instead, hold onto it until you are ready to begin receiving payments. You can defer payments until a later date, in which case your regular amount will be somewhat larger. For example, if you put off receiving your State Pension for a year after reaching eligibility, your weekly payments thereafter will increase by 10.4 per cent.

You also have the option of receiving the pension payments you deferred in a lump sum. (This option is available only if you defer State Pension for at least one year.) The total amount of State Pension you deferred will be totalled up and interest will be added at a rate 2 per cent higher than the current base rate set by the Bank of England. (For example, as I write this chapter, in May 2009, the bank's base rate is 0.5 per cent, so the interest you received will be figured at a rate of 2.5 per cent.) This lump sum payment will be taxable. If you take the lump sum route, your subsequent State Pension payments will *not* be increased.

Calculating exactly how big your lump sum payment or your increased State Pension payments might be if you defer pension payments is fairly complicated. The government offers a detailed booklet explaining how to perform the calculations, or you can speak to a pensions specialist who will walk you through the figures.

The deferral option may make sense for people who don't have an immediate need for State Pension income. For example, if you are in good health and enjoy your job, you may decide to stay working for one or a few years after you reach retirement age, in which case it may make sense to let your State Pension funds grow for your later benefit.

In any case, once you reach State Pension eligibility age – whether or not you choose to begin receiving pension payments – you are no longer required to make National Insurance contributions. If you keep working, your employer will stop making National Insurance deductions from your pay cheque – a nice little bonus to look forward to if you're among the many elders who plan to remain in the workforce for a while.

A word of warning about the State Pension system: the UK is an ageing society and the State Pension is an unfunded one. As such, there has to be some doubt as to whether it will continue in its present form for the indefinite future. It would therefore be a mistake to rely only on this one leg of the stool.

The Occupational or Employer/Company Pension

The second leg of your retirement stool is the occupational pension. It's a term that covers quite a wide range of plans. An occupational pension is any type of retirement scheme that is run by your employer (if it's a public sector scheme) or pension trustees working for your employer. It is funded by moneys deducted from your pay cheque, usually supplemented by contributions from your employer. Here it's important to note that the money is not always deducted from your pay cheque, and sometimes no employee contribution is required. Income you receive through an occupational pension scheme does not affect any money you are entitled to through your basic State Pension. (However, if your occupational pension scheme is contracted out, as I explained earlier, you will lose some or all of your additional State Pension [S2P] payments.)

Payments from an occupational pension usually begin either at age 60 or 65, depending on the particular scheme your employer has set up. Some schemes have scrapped any formal retirement date. You may be able to draw pension payments even if you continue working.

If you work for an employer who offers an occupational pension scheme that you are entitled to join, it's almost always a good idea to sign up. (Under current law, most companies with more than five employees are required to offer either an occupational pension scheme, a Group Personal Pension or access to a stakeholder pension scheme, a variation I'll explain later.) Currently, around 11 million people in the UK – almost half the workforce – are in occupational pension schemes, and those currently retiring with membership in such a scheme are among the wealthiest pensioners.

Signing up for your company's occupational pension scheme offers you several important benefits. First, your contributions are deducted from your pay cheque before tax is paid, which means that you get a tax break with every pound you contribute. Thus, if you pay the basic rate of income tax (20 per cent), for every £100 you pay into your occupational pension scheme, you'll save on that year's taxes. This is a good deal.

Second, most employers will make contributions to your fund on your behalf (check with the individual scheme to see how much your employer puts in). This is 'free money' that you would certainly be foolish to pass up. If you don't join, you are giving up your pay increase.

Third, many occupational pension plans provide other benefits to their members, such as life assurance or a pension for your dependants if you die. Again, the administrators of your company's plan can provide you with detailed information about the benefits they offer.

Up until April 2006 you were only allowed to invest up to 15 per cent of your salary in pension contributions. Those limits have now been abolished, although some pension schemes may impose their own limit on contributions. You may find that your employer adds another 5 per cent again (or more), which is not to be sniffed at.

There are two main types of occupational scheme: *final salary schemes* and *money-purchase schemes*.

Final Salary Schemes

With final salary schemes (also known as *salary-based, salary-related, superannuation, defined benefit* or *DB plans*), you know in advance how much income you will get in retirement. The payouts are generally based on the number of years you have been a member of the scheme and your average earnings in the last three years before you retire. (In some cases, only basic salary is counted in the 'final salary' calculation; in other cases, extras such as overtime pay and bonuses are included.) The proportion paid, known as the 'accrual rate', is often calculated as 1/60th or 1/80th of your final earnings for each year you've worked for the company.

For example, if Helen has been in a 1/60th scheme for 20 years, and her final salary is £30,000, her pension will be:

£30,000 ÷ 60 x 20 = £10,000 a year

This amount will normally be increased in line with prices for each year of retirement, and it's likely to be transferable to her spouse on her death.

With final salary schemes, the employer takes the responsibility for making sure that there is enough money in the pot when employees retire to pay off at the promised rate. Around 3.3 million people in the UK pay into schemes like these, and they provide a high degree of security and simplicity for people who are planning their retirements. It's comforting when you can calculate with some precision the amount of income you can expect from this second leg of your retirement stool.

Unfortunately, most companies that maintain final salary schemes are now closing them to new employees. (It is largely in the public sector that you find final salary schemes.) In times of stock market downturn, many firms consider final salary schemes too expensive to run. In fact, recent research by the consulting firm of Watson Wyatt shows that fully three quarters of UK firms with final salary plans are considering shifting to money-purchase plans or otherwise severing the link between pre-retirement salary and pension.

If you can still get into a final salary scheme, it's probably a good idea as long as you trust the company. If you work for a big corporation, or the health or education services or the civil service, you should be fine.

A Money-Purchase or Defined Contribution Plan

By contrast, if your company offers a money-purchase scheme (also known as a *defined contribution* or *DC scheme*) your retirement income can't be precisely calculated in advance. Instead, you accumulate your retirement fund over the year by contributing money from your salary and, in some cases, from matching contributions made by your employer. The retirement income you'll enjoy will depend on the amount of money you (and, if they do so, your employer) contributed, how well the investment fund has performed or grown over the years, and the investment costs and administrative charges.

When you retire, the investment fund will be divided up to provide you with a retirement package that has two parts. In most cases, you can choose to take up to 25 per cent of the fund as a tax-free lump sum. The remainder is used either to provide regular pension payments or to buy an *annuity* – a kind of insurance policy that provides a regular income for the rest of your life. The amount of monthly payments you'll receive depends on how much has been paid in by you and your employer, how well the fund has grown and (if applicable) the annuity rates on offer when you retire.

Another option is to transfer your occupational pension money-purchase scheme to a Self Invested Personal Pension (SIPP) where you can take the same 25 per cent then leave the other 75 per cent invested, but take either 120 per cent of a single life annuity as income, or zero, or anything in between.

Money-purchase pensions generally produce less generous results than final salary plans. In fact, recent research suggests that most workers covered under money-purchase plans should expect to have to supplement their retirement income from other sources – most often, a personal pension plan. In a 2007 study, the giant fund management firm Fidelity found that the average worker who has been saving for 40 years in a money-purchase plan is likely to have a post-retirement income of just 43 per cent of his or her final earnings. This is well below the 75 per cent that most retirees say they need, and even below the 50 per cent many people describe as the absolute minimum they must have to live on.

You can make contributions to a final salary occupational pension scheme of any amount up to 100 per cent of your salary or £245,000 a year (assuming the scheme lets you), and up to a lifetime maximum (currently set at £1.75 million). This applies to all pensions unless you have either Primary or Enhanced Protection (which means you can pay in more than the lifetime limit).

With all occupational schemes, someone else will be investing your money for you, so make sure you ask plenty of questions. Don't be passive. I'll tell you some of the questions to ask in coming chapters. I'll also offer advice on what to do if the company in which you've invested your retirement savings gets into trouble.

You should get regular statements (at least once a year) to tell you how well the fund is doing, so if it doesn't look as though your investments are growing fast enough you can supplement them through additional savings. Your employer may also be able to provide you with what is called a *combined pension forecast*. This shows the amount of income you can expect from both your State Pension and your occupational pension – two of the three legs of your stool. It's a convenient way to begin your analysis of where your retirement planning process currently stands. Ask your employer about whether this service is available to you.

As you can see, an occupational pension is tied to your job, which can be a double-edged sword. A generation or two ago, many workers stayed with the same company for a lifetime. Today, such loyalty is uncommon (in either direction), so you need to pay close attention to what happens to your occupational pension when you change employers. In some cases, you will be able to transfer your pension to your new company. In other cases, you may be able to keep your benefits under the old company's scheme while signing up with your new company's plan. Some workers who change jobs several times during a career may end up with small pensions from several different companies, all of which add up to a good-sized retirement nest egg. But such a complex arrangement requires careful monitoring.

If you've lost track of a pension scheme to which you contributed in a former job, you can probably dig up the information you need to figure out whether you will be entitled to payments after you retire. The government Pension Service offers a pension tracing service you can initiate by visiting this web page: http://www.thepensionservice.gov.uk/atoz/atozdetailed/pensiontracing.asp. Alternatively, you can telephone 0845 600 2537 and speak to an adviser who can help you launch the pension tracing process.

Another source of concern is company bankruptcies or

financial problems that may affect the funding of an occupational scheme. These are genuine issues that confront many thousands of workers every year. (It's one reason why the State Pension scheme remains an important element of the retirement planning process – after all, almost no private business, no matter how large or well run, is as financially secure as the British government.) We'll explain later what you need to do if your company, or a former employer, encounters financial troubles that might endanger your occupational pension.

Your Personal Pension Plan

Now on to the third leg of the stool – your personal pension plan. Not everyone needs a personal pension plan. For a lucky few, the combination of State Pension and an occupational pension will produce retirement income generous enough to ensure a comfortable lifestyle without work. But such people are relatively small in number. Most people, even those with both State Pensions and occupational pensions to look forward to, find that a personal retirement nest egg is necessary to enjoy the kind of post-work life they really want, as well as to cover them in case of unexpected expenses.

Personal or Private Pension Scheme

There are many ways of building a personal nest egg for retirement. One of the best is to create a *personal* or *private pension scheme*. This is a pension in your own name.

You buy a personal pension from a pension provider such as a bank, a building society or a life assurance company. Pensions have several built-in advantages as a way of saving money for retirement:

- You don't pay tax on money you put into pension funds. Thus, for basic rate taxpayers, each £1 added to their fund in effect costs them only 80p, while for higher rate taxpayers, £1 costs only 60p (although from April 2011 it's proposed that for those earning more than £150,000 a year, tax relief will be gradually reduced from 40 per cent, so those on more than £180,000 will only receive tax relief at 20 per cent).
- The profits made by your money while in the pension fund are tax-free, and you can take out a tax-free lump sum of up to 25 per cent of your total pension on retirement.
- The money is locked away, so you are not tempted to touch it before you reach 50, or 55 from 2010.
- You can usually choose the kinds of investments that your money goes towards.
- Your personal pension is not tied to a job or an employer. Thus, you can go on contributing to the pension after you change jobs or even if you stop working altogether.

No other method of investing for retirement provides you with all of these benefits. However, there are disadvantages to personal pension schemes as well. They include:

- You may lose money you've put in, since all investments have some degree of risk.
- Pension providers charge a management fee, and you need to keep an eye on how much this is cutting into your capital.
- Your money is locked away until you retire.

The key, then, is to choose your personal pension carefully and pay into it regularly, but don't rely on it alone to keep your head above water when you retire. Above all, as with any investment programme, keep an eye on the growth of your money, and make sensible changes if you're not achieving the results you need.

Payments from a personal pension may begin any time after the age of 50, depending on the rules of the particular scheme you belong to. (For most kinds of pensions, the minimum age fixed by law will rise to 55 in April 2010.) However, most people wait until age 60 or 65, so that their retirement savings can grow larger before they begin drawing moneys from the account. As with other kinds of pensions, you don't necessarily have to give up work to begin receiving benefits.

All private pension schemes are money-purchase schemes (even if they're called something different, such as a stakeholder pension), meaning you'll build up a lump sum of investment that you can use to buy an annuity or draw income from directly after you retire.

At one time, there were strict limits to the amount the government would let you salt away with the benefit of tax relief in your personal pension. The good news is that those limits have been greatly loosened, thanks to a series of pension reforms and simplifications effective from 6 April 2006 (now known as A-Day). The maximum you can pay into your pension each year is now 100 per cent of your earned income, up to a limit of £245,000 (rising to £255,000 by 2010), an amount so large that very few people can ever expect to bump up against it. There is also a lifetime limit of £1.75 million (rising to £1.8 million by April 2010). If you exceed this limit, the excess will be taxed at 25 per cent as you withdraw it, or at 55 per cent if you withdraw it as a lump sum.

These amounts could change in the future, of course. Your personal pension provider may ask for proof of your earnings, as they have a legal obligation to make sure you are not investing (and claiming tax relief on) too much. But remember: you can invest up to £3,600 per year without any earnings at all.

Self Invested Personal Pension (SIPP)

If you are confident about your own investment abilities, you can take out a *Self Invested Personal Pension* (SIPP). It will be administered by an insurance or finance company, but you will be free to choose the investments, whether shares, cash, bonds or commercial property. I do a version of this myself, but I wouldn't recommend it for an absolute beginner. Practise your investment skills on a few stock market transactions and see how confident you feel after a year or so. (I'll provide more guidance on this later, but there's much more advice on honing your investment abilities in my book *Save and Invest*.)

One of the pitfalls into which many well-intentioned people slip is failing to maintain their savings and investment programme. In fact, statistics show that up to one in three people who start private pension schemes stop paying into them within three years. Make sure this isn't you! One way to avoid the problem is by setting up a direct debit to take the money from your bank account every month, and then letting it run.

Are you unemployed? Even if you don't do paid work, you should still take steps to ensure you have a pension entitlement when you retire. You're going to find yourself in dire straits one day if you have no pension and not enough National Insurance contributions to entitle you to a full State Pension. The route you take depends on your personal circumstances:

- If you are married, make sure your spouse's pension will be paid to you if he or she dies first. This is crucial.
- Other people – husband, wife, parents, grandparents or generous friends – can pay up to £3,600 a year into a stakeholder pension on your behalf. Or you can do it yourself, if you have the money.

This makes a whole lot of sense for a non-working spouse because it can be very tax efficient. Let's say you save £3,600 per year for 20 years. This could become a fund of £120,000, if it grows at 5 per cent, which could then give a tax-free lump sum of £30,000, plus a tax-free income from the remaining £90,000. (This is because the tax-free allowance for people over 65 years of age is £9,030 per year.)

Remember, too, that if you care for someone who is long-term sick or disabled, or if you are incapacitated yourself in some way that prevents you from working, make sure the Department for Work and Pensions knows your situation so that you receive all the State Pension benefits to which you are entitled.

Are you a director running your own business? You could set up a SIPP or a SSAS (Small Self-Administered Scheme, which is an occupational version of a SIPP) for yourself. This allows you to make contributions from company profits, free of corporation tax, or to pay in personal contributions free of income tax. (Note: since A-Day you can only put in the equivalent of 100 per cent of your earnings or the annual limit, no matter what type of pension you invest in.) You can even hold some of the company's assets, such as the office premises, in a pension fund. Then the company would have to pay rent to the pension for the privilege of using the offices!

This scheme is a great way to build a pension plan fast, as long as your company can afford it. Get advice from your accountant and lawyer about how to set up such a plan so that it makes both financial and legal sense.

Some employers offer non-occupational pension schemes known as *group personal pensions* (GPPS). Don't be confused – although these are arranged through the company where you work, they are personal pensions, not occupational pensions, and your employer is not responsible for the financial results you obtain.

Group personal pensions are a collection of individual personal pensions bundled together and run by a pension provider, such as an insurance company or bank. Since 2001, your employer has been obliged to contribute 3 per cent of your annual salary to such schemes on your behalf if they do not want to set up a stakeholder pension and if it's the only pension scheme they offer. Contributions to the fund are taken from your salary after tax and HM Customs & Revenue pays the tax relief to your pension provider (though if you're a higher rate taxpayer, you'll have to claim it back on your tax return).

A group personal pension can be a good idea if your employer has managed to negotiate good terms with the pension provider, such as a bulk discount on fees, but note that these terms will probably cease if you change jobs. The pension should be transferable, but the terms may not be. As with occupational schemes, it would be a shame to turn down the offer of additional contributions from your employer, but research the company running the scheme and ask hard questions.

Finally, there are *stakeholder pensions*, a new type of personal pension introduced in 2001. They offer most of the same benefits as other personal pensions, including tax relief on the money you invest and independence from any employer. One major difference, however, is that management charges with a stakeholder pension are capped at 1.5 per cent of the value of the fund each year for the first ten years and 1 per cent thereafter. This is less than you pay with most other personal pensions.

The stakeholder pension is also very flexible, for example, minimum payments are low (currently just £20 per month) and there are no penalties if you miss a payment. You can save what you want, when you want, or take a break from saving if you have a period of unemployment. You can switch from one scheme to another without incurring charges.

Stakeholder pensions are available to anyone under the age of 75, a resident in the UK, who is either not eligible for an occupational or employer-based pension scheme, or who wants to top up their employer pension or save for their retirement if they are not earning (perhaps because they are caring for the family or receiving rental income from property).

If you decide to take out a stakeholder pension organised by your employer, they will be able to deduct contributions from your pay. This is a valuable benefit, since regular saving is the best and easiest way to build up a sizeable nest egg with little effort on your part. However, your employer does not have to make any additional contributions on your behalf. Don't automatically opt for an employer's scheme if they're not contributing; shop around and you might well find a better deal on your own. Both stakeholders and GPPs are money-purchase schemes, meaning the amount you get at retirement depends on how the fund has grown and on charges made on the fund.

This is just a brief outline of the types of pension available. It should be clear to you by now which one will be most suitable for your circumstances. If you are considering a stakeholder pension, the FSA website has a 'decision tree' – a list of questions that will help you to make up your mind.

There are other ways to save beyond the pension options. For example, tax-free Individual Savings Accounts (ISAs) offer a number of advantages and are worth considering. An ISA is a special kind of account designed to let you save without paying tax on the growth of your savings. It's not in itself a savings vehicle but rather a 'wrapper' that can hold various kinds of savings or investment products, from savings accounts to shares to bonds. The interest from a cash ISA and growth of a stocks and shares ISA are free of income tax and capital gains tax respectively, and you don't have to declare an ISA on your tax return. [Note: income taxes are automatically paid on dividends earned within the ISA fund, so they're not so tax efficient for basic rate taxpayers.]

Each tax year, you can put a total of £7,200 into ISAs. (This will rise to £10,200 for those aged 50 and over from October 2009, and for everyone from April 2010). You can have either a cash ISA or a stocks and shares ISA or one of each in any one tax year (a tax year runs from 6 April of one year to 5 April of the next).

There are two basic kinds of investments that can go into an ISA:

- **Cash ISA:** a cash ISA may include an ISA bank or building society account or some other kinds of savings accounts specially designed for ISAs. In any given year, you can invest up to £3,600 in a cash mini ISA (rising to £5,100 by 2010 at the latest).

- **Stocks and shares ISA:** a stocks and shares mini ISA may include shares in companies, corporate bonds, government bonds (gilts), unit trusts, investment trusts or investment funds. (We'll discuss all these investment vehicles in the next chapter.) In any given year, you can invest a total of up to £7,200 into a stocks and shares ISA (£10,200 by 2010). You don't have to invest the lot in stocks and shares if you don't want to. You can split your contribution so up to £3,600 is held in a cash ISA (£5,100 by 2010) and the rest in a stocks and shares ISA.

If you already have money in a cash ISA from previous tax years, you can transfer some or all of it into a stocks and shares ISA and it will not affect your annual allowance. You can get an ISA from an ISA manager, which is an organisation approved by HMRC and authorised by the FSA. ISA managers include banks, building societies, investment firms and stockbrokers. Not all ISA managers offer all kinds of ISAs. So if you want to pay your ISA savings into various kinds of savings and investment plans, you may want to use more than one ISA manager. There's no problem with this at all.

What type of ISA is best for you? It depends on many factors. In later chapters of this book, I'll explain how to think about different kinds of investments and how to decide what forms of investments make sense for you based on your age, your financial goals, your personal risk tolerance and other considerations. For now, I'll offer the following rules of thumb:

- Most people need a basic cash reserve to protect them against emergency needs. For this purpose a cash ISA is best. A good rule of thumb is to keep six to nine months of your usual monthly income (or monthly expenses) in cash, and preferably in a cash ISA. In more stable economic times, you should keep three to six months' income.
- Consider investing retirement savings in a stocks and shares ISA. This kind of investment vehicle carries greater risk than a cash ISA, but it usually offers a potential higher rate of growth over a long time period.

You pay no income tax on any interest you get from your ISA, except dividends from a stocks and shares ISA are taxed at 20 per cent. In addition, your ISA is free from capital gains tax. This is tax that is normally payable on any increase in value in a share or unit trust investment. Finally, you don't have to list your ISAs on your UK tax form.

If you've reached your annual limit on ISA payments, consider using one of the National Savings and Investments' products as an additional source of tax-free money growth. These are tax-free forms of saving that include Fixed and Index-linked Savings Certificates and Premium Bonds. They don't need to be listed on your tax return. You can invest in these tax-free on top of any amounts you put away in an ISA – even if you've reached the limit of your allowable ISA payment for the year.

In addition, other forms of investment, such as property and a business you own, may play a role in your retirement savings plan.

Mapping out Your Individual Savings Plan

Now that you have a general sense of how the three legs of your retirement stool work, you're ready for the next important step in the planning process – estimating how much income you can expect from your government and occupational pensions. That calculation will put you in a position to figure out the size of the gap that needs to be filled by an individual savings plan.

Here's a simple example of how to perform such a calculation. Howard and Diane Mason are a married couple aged 51 and 45 respectively. They both work, Howard as a mid-level corporate manager with an annual income of £48,000, Diane as a pharmaceutical sales rep earning £32,000 per year. Howard hopes to either stop working or drastically reduce his workload around the time he turns 65, which is the same time they will finish paying off their home mortgage. Diane may or may not continue working at that point (she'll be 59 then).

Having worked through the Retirement Expense Planning, the Masons' best estimate is that they will need an income of about £4,000 per month after they retire, which amounts to £48,000 per year.

Now they need to consider the amount of income they can expect. First, the Masons call the Retirement Pension Forecasting team at the Pension Service to get an estimate of the government pension they'll receive. The amount that's forecast is about £200 per week, which translates into roughly £870 per month (a little over £10,000 per year).

Second, they check with the pension administrators at the companies where they work to find out how much their pensions will pay. The total turns out to be another £1,500 per month (£18,000 per year).

The total from government and private pensions of £2,370 per month leaves a gap of £1,630 that the Masons need to fill from savings (close to £20,000 per year). How large a personal pension will it take to produce that kind of income?

Here is where some economic guesswork is needed. Let's suppose that, on retirement, the Masons can put their savings into an investment fund that grows by around 5 per cent per year. This is a reasonably conservative assumption. The Masons will want to live entirely on this 5 per cent growth rather than shrinking their savings each year.

To calculate the size of the nest egg needed to produce the desired income, the Masons have to do a little maths. Here's the formula:

X is the size of the nest egg the Masons will need.
.05 is the annual growth rate the Masons are assuming for
   their money (since .05 is the same as 5 per cent).
£20,000 is the annual income they want.
X times .05 = 20,000.
To find the value of X, divide both sides of the equation by
   .05.
So X = £20,000 divided by .05.
Using a calculator to divide £20,000 by .05, the Masons find
   that X = £400,000.
So the Masons need a nest egg of £400,000 to produce the
   annual income they want.

The process of figuring out how much money you need to save in order to enjoy the retirement you want can be daunting, not because the calculations are complicated – as the example demonstrates, they are really simple – but because it's scary to see the price tag of your dreams reduced to an unyielding, black-and-white number. Don't be afraid. Go ahead and perform the calculation.

You can calculate the size of the nest egg you'll need by following the same steps. In place of '£20,000' in the formula, substitute the amount of annual income you need to generate for your retirement. If you are happy to eat into some of your capital to produce income, you will not need such a large nest egg. You can use the same 5 per cent growth assumption (.05) or change it – for example, to make the formula even more conservative and cautious, you could assume 4 per cent growth (.04). Once you know the height of the mountain you need to climb, you can begin developing realistic plans for achieving the summit. One thing is certain – unless you know your destination, the odds of reaching it are poor.

In the remainder of this book, I'll show you how to create a savings and investment plan that will help you realise your retirement dreams. I'll explain how to find money from your daily budget to begin a savings programme, even if you think you feel too financially stressed to afford one. I'll teach you the basics you need to know about saving and investing, including a primer on investment risk – how to avoid excessive risk and how to make reasonable levels of risk work in your favour. And I'll also show you how to keep tabs on the other two legs of your retirement stool – your government pension and your occupational pension – so that, by the time you're ready to retire, all three legs will be secure and solid.

When you're ready to begin, take a deep breath and turn to the next chapter.

4. 'Who Has Money to Save?' You Do

Launch Your Savings Programme – the Sooner the Better

If you've followed all the steps I've walked you through so far, you've come a long way on the path to creating a powerful retirement plan. You've put flesh and bones on what may once have been vague dreams about the kind of life you'd like to live after retirement, and you've estimated the amount of money it will take to make those dreams come true. You've also checked into the current status of your three-legged retirement stool, having figured out the kinds of payments (if any) you can expect to receive from the government, and from your current and past employers when retirement age rolls around. Finally, you've measured the gap between the money you need for a comfortable retirement and the money you'll be receiving from the first two legs of your stool.

Now it's time to begin building the third leg – a personal retirement savings plan that will fill that gap and turn a possibly insecure future into one you can look forward to with confidence.

And here is where you may find yourself becoming a little nervous – because changes in your current habits may be necessary. For many people, saving money is a real challenge, and I'm not going to pretend it isn't.

You may want to protest that right now is not a good time for you to launch a savings programme. Maybe you don't know where to put your money because banks, property and the investment markets are too risky during the current financial crisis. Maybe you're trying to pay off your student loan, or the bills from a wedding, or saving a deposit to buy a flat or a house. Maybe you're expecting a baby later this year, or you've just been hit with unexpected bills to fix your car or your cooker or your roof. Maybe you want to tuck away any spare cash in order to start that business you've always dreamed of. And then there's that once-in-a-lifetime holiday you and your friends have been planning.

Some of these are all excellent ways to use your money and I don't want to discourage you from making these kinds of plans. But it's a mistake to use any of these short-term goals as an excuse to put off saving for retirement, even when the financial world seems about to implode. And believe me, that's what it is – an excuse. There will always be something (more likely, several things) to spend your pay cheques on that is more fun, inspiring and immediate than retirement. If you go on allowing these worthy causes to get in the way of retirement planning, you'll soon find yourself pushing 40 . . . then 45 . . . then 50 . . . and 50-ish . . . and before you know it, retirement will be staring you in the face and you'll have nothing in your account except a pile of IOUs you've written to yourself.

Facing up to the need to start saving is especially hard for young people. There are many reasons for this. Twenty-somethings want to party; they've usually just finished college and are probably enjoying the first grown-up pay cheques of their lives, along with the freedom of their new-found independence. Under the circumstances, there are a million things they'd rather do with their money than save it. What's more, retirement age seems very distant when you're just starting out. And, of course, when you're working at your first or second job, it's quite likely that your salary is rather small, which makes the idea of putting away part of it every week especially difficult. All these factors make retirement saving a low priority for most young people.

I have to own up and tell you that I didn't start a pension scheme in my early 30s. Having graduated from college – the first person in my family to do so – and moved from my family home in a rural corner of the American South to the glamour of a big, vibrant city, I threw myself headlong into the excitement of urban life. I discovered the allure of the credit card, which let me buy clothes and drinks and dinners and holidays even when my bank account was practically empty. I ended up spending every penny I earned – and even a little bit more. So I understand the psychology of those who are putting off starting their retirement planning. I've been there and done that – and now I'm writing the book!

And while I won't deny that I enjoyed the heady pleasures of over-spending (if they weren't delightful, no one would have a problem avoiding them), I must admit that I regret it now. I don't regret the fun I had in my 20s and early 30s – the stylish clothes, the nights on the town, and the travel to places I couldn't really afford – but I now realise that, with just a bit of foresight and self-control, I could have enjoyed 80 to 90 per cent of the same extravagances *and also* begun a long-term savings plan a decade sooner than I actually did.

And if I had, my finances today would be in better shape than they are. I'm not crying poverty, mind you – I expect to retire on schedule and comfortably. But to make this possible I've had to scrimp and sacrifice just a little more than I would have liked in order to compensate for those lost years of my 20s and early 30s. Here is a secret for you 20-somethings: when you get to be 35 and 40 and 50 years old, you will still find just as many enjoyable treats and goodies to spend your money on as you do today! So don't go crazy with spending now, in the old saying, 'as if there's no tomorrow'. There *is* a tomorrow, and a little sacrifice today will save you from having to sacrifice a lot tomorrow.

I have a rule of thumb calculation I sometimes use to illustrate the value of starting your retirement saving early. To estimate the percentage of your salary you should be saving for retirement, take the age at which you *begin* your savings programme and divide it in half. Thus:

- If you start saving at age 22, you should save 11 per cent of your salary.
- If you start at 30, you should save 15 per cent.
- If you start at 40, you should save 20 per cent.
- And if you don't start until you are 50, you will need to invest 25 per cent of your salary every year to build a comfortable retirement package – one pound in every four.

Importantly, the percentages above include any money you are contributing to your work pension and State Pension. If you want to be more conservative, exclude the contributions you make to your State Pension.

Like every rule of thumb, this is only an approximation. As you work your way through the rest of this book, you'll come up with more precise figures as to what you need to save. But the principle is valid: the longer you wait to begin, the more arduous your climb to the pinnacle of a happy retirement will be.

The Beauty of Compound Interest

Of course, any task is easier when you have more time to perform it. But there's a special reason why saving is much easier when you start earlier. It's an almost magical effect known as *compound interest*. Here's how it works.

As you know, when you deposit money in a savings account the bank pays you interest on your money at a rate expressed as a percentage of the amount you save. For example, 6 per cent interest would be six pounds for every hundred pounds in your account (although you would probably have to pay income tax at 20 per cent or 40 per cent on the interest, we will ignore that in this example). This is like 'free money', a kind of gift from the bank (which comes from the profits the bank makes on its own investments, funded by depositors like you). This is a wonderful benefit of saving – but it's only the start of the story.

Compound interest is money from the bank that is paid not only on the amount you've deposited but also *on the interest you've already earned*. In effect, it is 'interest paid on interest' – which means, as your account grows, the speed at which your money grows steadily increases.

Here is an example. Suppose you deposit £100 in a savings account that yields 6 per cent interest, compounded annually (that is, once a year). After one year, your £100 will have increased by 6 per cent. That's the equivalent of multiplying it by 1.06 (which is the same as adding 6 per cent):

£100 x 1.06 = £106

So your savings account will grow in year one by six pounds. So far, so good. Now, what will happen in year two? If the same 6 per cent interest applies, your savings will grow by *more* than six pounds – because you will earn interest on the total amount in your account, which is now £106:

£106 x 1.06 = £112.36

In year two, the interest you earn is £12.36, the extra 36 pence due to compounding.

The effect may not be very impressive so far, but as time passes, it becomes more and more striking, as the chart overleaf shows.

The Effect of Compound Interest
(6 per cent per year, compounded annually)

End of Year	Account Balance
1	£106.00
2	£112.36
3	£119.10
4	£126.25
5	£133.82
6	£141.85
7	£150.36
8	£159.38
9	£168.95
10	£179.08
11	£189.83
12	£201.22
13	£213.29
14	£226.09
15	£239.66
16	£254.04
17	£269.28
18	£285.43
19	£302.56
20	£320.71
21	£339.96
22	£360.35
23	£381.97
24	£404.89
25	£429.19
26	£454.94
27	£482.23
28	£511.17
29	£541.84
30	£574.35

Notice what happens. In the first few years, compounding gives you just a few extra pence. But as your account grows, so does the power of compound interest. By year ten, your original £100 is earning over £11 of interest (£6 due to the basic 6 per cent rate, more than £5 extra due to compounding). By year 20, you are earning £18 of interest. And in year 30, your £100 is earning more than £30 of interest. What's more, the amount of your savings has grown with time to over £574 – a more than five-fold increase, with no effort on your part!

Now you see why we call this the 'beauty of compound interest'. Our financial system is set up to make *time work for you*. The longer you let your money grow, the bigger it will grow – and the easier it will be to accumulate a really significant amount of savings.

Also notice in the example on page 72 that we have *not* added a single penny to the original £100 investment. In reality, any good savings programme will involve regular deposits into the account. Imagine how quickly the account shown above would grow if another £100 were added each year beginning the first year! Actually, don't imagine – here are the numbers:

The Effect of Compound Interest
(6 per cent per year, compounded annually, with £100 deposited each year)

End of Year	Account Balance
1	£206.00
2	£318.36
3	£437.46
4	£563.71
5	£697.53
6	£839.38
7	£989.75
8	£1,149.13
9	£1,318.08

End of Year	Account Balance
10	£1,497.16
11	£1,686.99
12	£1,888.21
13	£2,101.51
14	£2,327.60
15	£2,567.25
16	£2,821.29
17	£3,090.56
18	£3,376.00
19	£3,678.59
20	£3,999.27
21	£4,339.23
22	£4,699.58
23	£5,081.56
24	£5,486.45
25	£5,915.64
26	£6,370.57
27	£6,852.81
28	£7,363.98
29	£7,905,82
30	£8,480.17

Thanks to compound interest, savings of just £100 per year – a trifle, really – amounts to well over £8,000 after 30 years. And if you allow even more time for your savings to grow – as you will if you start in your 20s – the positive impact will be even greater.

This is why – along with every responsible financial adviser – I place so much emphasis on *starting young*. The amount you will need to save for a comfortable retirement is probably a daunting sum – in the hundreds of thousands, if not the millions of pounds. It might seem impossible – and for most people, it *would* be impossible if not for the power of compound interest. Start saving today so that this power will have plenty of time to work on your behalf.

One other point: although I emphasise how valuable it is to start your retirement savings programme as early as possible – preferably in your 20s – I don't mean to discourage you if you've already reached middle age, or to imply that you have no opportunity to prepare for a satisfying retirement in your 40s or 50s. If you are within 20 years of retirement age, don't give up hope! With some smart planning and a serious effort at marshalling your resources, you can still arrange for a comfortable post-work lifestyle – and the sooner you start, the better.

Setting a Savings Goal

I hope I've convinced you that beginning to save for retirement as soon as possible is a good idea, at least in theory. But how do you transform it into a practical reality, in a world where plenty of other demands are competing for your pounds – and your priorities?

The first step is to decide on a savings goal. At the end of chapter 3, I walked you through an example (based on the life of Howard and Diane Mason) of how to calculate the size of the retirement nest egg you need to serve as the third leg of your stool. If you haven't already done so, perform the calculation now based on your own circumstances. Contact the Retirement Pension Forecasting Team to find out how much income you can expect to receive from your government pension. Also contact the administrators of your company pension (if you have one) to learn the expected payout from the second leg of the stool. Add these amounts together (including income from both you and your partner, if any) to determine your retirement income from government and company sources.

Then turn back to the end of chapter 2, where you estimated the amount of income you will need to live the retirement lifestyle you desire. The difference between this figure and your estimated retirement income will be the amount you need to produce from your personal savings.

Now use the same formula the Masons used in chapter 3 to calculate the size of the savings nest egg you will need to generate the income you want. You will have to decide on a percentage that represents the income you expect to receive from your investments at the time you retire. Just as with estimating future inflation, this figure is impossible to predict with certainty. You might consider using 5 per cent (equivalent to .05) as a reasonable amount, with 6 per cent (.06) as a more optimistic figure, 4 per cent (.04) as a more conservative, cautious one.

Divide the amount of annual income you need to generate by the percentage you choose, and the result will be the size of the savings nest egg you need. So, if you find that you need an annual income from personal savings of £27,500 and you decide to use 5 per cent as your income projection, the calculation will look like this:

£27,500 ÷ .05 = £550,000

So you will need a nest egg of £550,000 to generate the income required to make up the third leg of your retirement stool. Now, how much money do you need to start saving today in order to have £550,000 in your account by the time you retire? There are several ways to calculate this.

One way is to simply divide the total amount of your desired nest egg by the number of years you have until retirement. This will give you an annual savings goal. For example, if you're 39 years old, you're probably 26 years from retirement (assuming the usual retirement age of 65). If you want a nest egg of £550,000 and you are starting from zero, you can calculate the amount to save like this:

£550,000 ÷ 26 = £21,154

According to this formula, you will need to save a little over £21,000 every year in order to amass £550,000 by age 65. That's just under £1,800 per month.

Of course, this formula is overly-simple in that it *ignores* the interest you will earn on your savings. As we've seen, the power of compound interest is so great that this is a big omission! If you follow this overly-simple formula and deposit your savings in any interest-bearing bank account, you will end up with *more* money than predicted. That's a good thing!

However, if you want to calculate the amount you need to save more accurately (taking interest into account), the computations required are a little more difficult. One way to estimate the amount is by using a *compound interest calculator.* This is an automated computer program that quickly calculates how your money will grow at a specified interest rate. You can easily find such programs on the Internet* or by consulting an adviser at your nearest bank.

Using a compound interest calculator to estimate the amount you need to save for retirement may take a few steps. Here's an example. Knowing we need to accumulate a nest egg of £550,000, we turned to a compound interest calculator on the Internet and keyed in the numbers requested. (Every compound interest calculator looks a little different, but they all ask for much the same information.)

CURRENT PRINCIPAL:	£0.00
ANNUAL ADDITION:	£15,000.00
YEARS TO GROW:	26
INTEREST RATE:	5%

CALCULATE

FUTURE VALUE:	£805,036.90

---

* One easy-to-use compound interest calculator is available on the website of the Motley Fool investment advice organisation, at www.fool.co.uk. Another can be found at www.ft.com.

'Current principal' is the amount we have in savings now. Assuming that we are starting from scratch, we filled in zero.

'Annual addition' is the amount we will save each year. As a guess, we filled in £15,000.

'Years to grow' is the length of time we have to build our savings account. Since we are 26 years from retirement, we filled in that number.

'Interest rate' is the rate at which we expect our money to grow. We decided to use the moderate rate of 5 per cent.

Having filled in all these numbers, we clicked on the 'Calculate' button and got the future value of our nest egg, as of age 65, of £805,036.90.

Now, this is *more* than the £550,000 we are aiming for. Again, it's never a problem to have *more* money. But this shows us that we don't have to save as much as £15,000 every year to end up with savings of £550,000. So we returned to the online calculator and changed our estimated annual savings amount, this time keying in the amount of £10,000. Then we pressed the 'Calculate' button. Now the computer screen looked like this:

CURRENT PRINCIPAL:	£0.00
ANNUAL ADDITION:	£10,000.00
YEARS TO GROW:	26
INTEREST RATE:	5%

CALCULATE

FUTURE VALUE:	£536,691.26

Aha! This is pretty close to our £550,000 target. We could go on experimenting – for example, trying £11,000 as the annual savings amount – or simply choose a figure that makes sense. For instance, we could decide to round up and use £12,000 per year as our savings goal, since that gives us a nice round number of £1,000 per month to save.

This, of course, is just an example. For some people, the size of the required nest egg may be considerably higher, such as for someone who is accustomed to a very comfortable lifestyle or has some large, unusual living expenses to manage. For other people, it may be smaller, such as for someone with a modest way of life or with an unusually generous company pension plan. And the number of years you have to save will make a big difference in how much you need to set aside every year. It goes without saying that accumulating half a million pounds over 40 years is a lot less difficult than accumulating the same amount in ten years.

But no matter what your personal circumstances are, the basic process is much the same: figure out the amount of savings you need to generate the income you'll require after you retire, and then calculate the sum you must save every year in order to reach that goal. You might want to figure out what percentage of your after-tax income this amount represents. (It can be handy to have a rule of thumb in mind when windfalls or bonuses come your way: 'I always save 12 per cent of every pound I earn.')

Now you can begin to figure out how you need to adjust your lifestyle and your spending habits to make that kind of saving possible.

Making Saving Simple

For most people, saving money is a little like getting physically fit: it's a fine idea we honestly intend to pursue, but very difficult to practise diligently every day.

Fortunately, there are some tricks and techniques you can use that will make saving money quite a bit simpler (and less psychologically taxing!) than going on a strict diet or working out at the gym. Here are some of the most useful tips I know that can help you turn saving from a 'nice idea' into a real part of your everyday life.

Put savings first. One of the main reasons most of us fail to save is that we try to save out of the money that is *left over* after other expenses have been covered. When the weekly, bi-weekly or monthly pay cheque arrives, we pay our bills, spend some money on things we need or want and set aside a little for daily use. Only then do we look at the dwindling pile of cash as a possible source of savings – and all too often find there is little or nothing there.

To escape this syndrome, *reverse* the process. Set aside your targeted savings percentage *first*, as soon as you get your pay cheque, and deposit it immediately into your savings account. Does this sound painful? At first, it may be. For a month or two, it will feel as if you've had your salary cut and you probably won't like it, but in time – for most people, surprisingly quickly – you'll become accustomed to living on the smaller amount. And you'll have the pleasure of watching your savings grow every month.

Arrange for automatic withdrawals. An even easier way of putting savings first is by signing up for a regular savings plan. Most banks will be happy to arrange for automatic withdrawals from your current account (say, by standing order or direct debit) into a special savings account. You can decide the amount to be transferred to savings and change it whenever you want. This will make your savings grow with no effort on your part and virtually eliminate the temptation to spend rather than save, since you will never 'see' the money that automatically flows into the savings account.

Save your next pay rise. Earmark your next pay increase for savings. After all, you've been living all right on your current income – just keep your lifestyle the same and enjoy a painless boost in your savings rate. If you find this too difficult, try a compromise: designate half or two-thirds of your next pay rise for savings and use the remainder to enhance your current lifestyle.

Save your bonuses, windfalls, gifts and other 'extras'. When money 'falls out of the sky' in the form of an unusual or un-expected windfall, it is tempting to spend it all on a shopping spree, a holiday getaway or a big night out with your friends. Resist the temptation! (Can you remember what you spent your *last* bonus on? If not, that's a good sign that whatever you squandered the money on wasn't particularly memorable or worthwhile!) Instead, tuck that windfall cheque away in your savings account – or, if you can't quite bring yourself to do that, save at least half.

Don't dip into your retirement savings. When you see your savings account growing month by month, you may be tempted to smash the piggy bank and use the funds for some immedi-ately-gratifying project. Resist the temptation! Remember that your savings programme will suffer in four ways if you dip into the account. First, the amount you've saved will, of course, imme-diately fall. Second, you'll spend the next several months labouring to get back to where you were, which is a highly discouraging, demotivating situation to face. Third, you'll lose the time advantage that compound interest creates, since having, say, £5,000 in the bank in January is worth much more in the long run than having that same amount six or eight months later. And fourth, by succumbing to the temptation to ransack your account once, you create a precedent that will make it more likely you'll do the same in the future – whereas an unblem-ished record of many years without touching the account creates a powerful aura of sanctity that grows with every passing month.

Don't touch your retirement savings unless a true emergency forces you to – by which I mean something like a leaking roof or a smashed-up car that you have *no* other way to fix. An incredible sale at the local department store or a fantastic deal on a Caribbean trip does *not* qualify as an emergency!

Open a limited access account. This is a special savings account that permits just a few withdrawals every year. A penalty is often imposed on withdrawals above the specified maximum. Keeping your retirement savings in a limited access account reduces the temptation to raid the funds whenever you have a special need or want. And it's a surprisingly effective way of forcing yourself to leave your money alone and let it grow.

Maybe it feels a little silly to try to 'trick' yourself into saving. Actually, all you are doing is creating circumstances in which the savings habit will have a better chance of growing. It's the same principle a would-be dieter follows when he or she stocks the refrigerator with fruits, veggies and healthful snacks rather than cakes, pies and ice cream. Once you become accustomed to saving – and to enjoying the sensation of watching your savings balance steadily increase – you'll find it easy to stay on track with your savings programme.

You could also save or, more accurately, invest into a plan that demands regular payments, such as an endowment plan. Although it will mean you're disciplined about your savings, there are serious downsides, so I wouldn't recommend it.

Sealing the Debt Drain

For many people, the biggest obstacle to saving is the burden of debt they're carrying. Large payments to credit card companies, holders of second mortgages, store card providers and other credit providers make up a large portion of their monthly spending. What's worse, these payments usually consist mainly of interest on the debt, so that the amount owed on the original purchase – the *capital* – scarcely shrinks from one month to the next. Trying to save in circumstances like these is like trying to bail out water from a boat while more water keeps pouring in through a hole in the bottom: no matter how much you scramble, the situation gets worse and worse.

If, like many, you are saddled with too much debt, you owe

it to yourself to get the problem under control. How much is 'too much'? If you can't set aside 10 per cent of your income for savings off the top every month *and* pay off your credit card debts in full every month, then you are letting debt control your financial future – and that means you owe too much.

There's no completely painless way to escape the debt demon. Part of the formula *must* be spending less money on non-essential purchases. Here are some elements of a debt-relief plan that can make the process, if not painless, at least simple and manageable.

Review your spending patterns – and change them. Pull out your last six months' worth of credit card bills and spend half an hour adding up your spending in various categories – clothes, home furnishings, meals and drinks, toys and gadgets, holidays, entertainment and so on. Look for areas of excess. You may be shocked to realise how much you've been spending on one or two favourite indulgences.

Once you identify the problem areas, make a realistic plan to get them under control. Don't expect to cut your spending to zero. Instead, decide how far back you can trim your spending without feeling completely deprived. For instance, if you find you've been spending hundreds of pounds on dining out, you might decide to limit yourself to two nights out per week. If clothes are your weakness, you might plan on buying one new outfit every month. Develop a plan, make a mental commitment to carrying it out and stick to it.

And don't let one or two lapses derail you permanently; if you slip up and overspend one weekend, forgive yourself and get back on track the following week. Resolve to follow any step backwards with at least two steps forward. If you do, you'll keep making progress towards your ultimate savings goal.

Reduce your credit card habit. First, cut back on the number of cards you hold. Having one or two major credit cards is useful and harmless. But one or two cards will suffice – there's no need to sport the array of five or ten cards I see many people carrying. The more card accounts you have, the greater your ability to rack up debt, and the more difficult it will be to save. I recommend you avoid credit cards issued by stores altogether. They generally charge the highest interest rates of any credit cards.

When you do use a credit card, pay off the balance in full every month. This means spending each month only what you can afford to pay for that month. If you're in doubt as to how much you've spent, you can call the phone number provided by the credit card company to get your balance. (I'm always stunned to discover how many people don't realise they can do this.) If your balance is running high, force yourself to postpone the next purchase until another month has passed. Otherwise, you'll find yourself with a bill you can't pay and an ever-mounting pile of interest-bearing debt.

Reduce the interest you pay. Take advantage of your credit card's interest-free grace period. This period exists only on purchases, not cash advances. The grace period may range in length from 0 to 55 days, depending on when your next month's bill comes due. At the end of the grace period, interest charges kick in. So the best money-saving strategy is to buy at the beginning of the grace period and pay off your purchase in full just before the end of the grace period. Payment must be made at the credit card company's offices by the end of the grace period, and it can take two to four days for the money to be credited to your account. Jot down in your personal diary or calendar the date of any large purchase you make so you can mail your payment at least seven days before the end of the grace period. It may be a better idea to pay your bill over the telephone or Internet. At least then you won't be at the mercy of the post.

This is one of the advantages of cutting back on the number of cards you hold. It's easy to keep track of the grace periods on one or two cards. When you have several cards, this strategy is likely to become too complicated to follow.

More Psychological Tips for Staying on Track with Savings

It's very possible that you have been finding this chapter stressful reading. Even *thinking about* changing your spending and saving habits can be challenging! Money is an emotional issue for many people, one that is deeply intertwined with our sense of self-worth, our feelings of satisfaction and deprivation, and our attitudes towards life itself. I understand these issues, having grappled with them myself, as well as helping many other people to recognise and cope with their impact.

So far, I've focused on practical strategies for improving your financial habits and getting started with a solid savings programme. Now let me offer a few psychological tips – techniques that many people have found helpful in dealing with the mental and emotional aspects of over-spending and under-saving.

Get healthy. One of the more surprising connections that researchers have discovered is between good health and financial success. For example, economist Jay Zagorsky at Ohio State University in the US has found that even a modest weight loss, reducing an individual from slightly overweight to normal, is accompanied by an average increase of 37 per cent in personal wealth. Lose more weight and the financial benefits are even greater. Similarly, economists Charles Baum and William Ford at Middle Tennessee State University have discovered that people with slender physiques earn on average 3 per cent (men) and 6 per cent (women) more than overweight individuals.

No one really knows *why* healthier people do better financially. Perhaps having a slimmer physique and feeling stronger and more energetic creates improved self-esteem; and perhaps this, in turn, reduces the need some people feel to use 'binge spending' as a way of beating the blues. Whatever the reason, the connection between physical and economic wellbeing is real.

So, as part of your personal financial makeover you might want to consider adopting a fitness regime as well.

In any case, being fit produces many direct financial benefits. People who quit smoking, cut their drinking and start exercising can dramatically reduce their vulnerability to a wide range of diseases from cancer and heart disease to diabetes, asthma and high blood pressure. As a result, they spend less time in the hospital, miss work less frequently, and trim the amount they must spend on life and health insurance (to say nothing of the money they save by reducing or eliminating the weekly bills for cigarettes and booze!).

Reward yourself for saving. As with dieting or exercise, some people find it hard to save simply because it smacks of self-denial, suffering or even punishment. These people may have been raised in families where money or material goods were used as symbols of love or rewards for good behaviour. Thus, as adults, they associate saving money and being frugal with being judged and rejected, an almost intolerable psychological burden.

If you suffer from this syndrome, try combating it by *reversing* your financial psychology. Create a new system of rewards in which wise spending patterns (rather than bouts of expensive self-indulgence) create a feeling of wellbeing. For example, you can set yourself one or more short-term savings goals: 'I'll put away four hundred pounds every month, for a total of four thousand eight hundred pounds a year.' Then reward yourself with some pleasurable treat each time you successfully reach a predetermined milestone. So every month that you add £400 to your savings account, you are 'allowed' to buy a new outfit or spend £40 at your favourite store, and every six months that the same goal is reached, you can take a long weekend holiday with your spouse, partner or best friend.

After a year or two of living under this new regime, you'll find yourself starting to associate saving with pleasure rather than with deprivation.

Change your frames of reference. Another psychological difficulty for many people is their tendency to compare their spending with that of other people – often people who are (or appear) much more affluent than they are. If you've developed this habit, you may find yourself justifying your excessive spending with remarks like, 'Oh, why shouldn't I take a week in Majorca – all my friends have been there already!' or, 'I *have* to buy that racy little sports car – nobody wants to be seen in an old clunker like the one I've been driving!'

One way to combat this tendency is to focus on the hard facts of the situation. Is it really true that 'all your friends' have been to Majorca – or are you really talking about the woman in accounting who is constantly bragging about her holiday trips? Is it a fact that 'nobody' can stand your four-year-old car – or are you focusing on and embellishing a sarcastic remark your snooty cousin made the last time you picked him up at the train station?

If you find yourself driven to overspend by actual or imagined peer pressure, remember that it's almost impossible to know the true financial status of our friends, relatives and neighbours, or the trade-offs they may have made in order to enjoy the flashy or luxurious lifestyle others observe. Yes, your office mate in the next cubicle may wear nicer suits than you – but is it possible he's been borrowing thousands of pounds from his elderly mum to pay his tailor bills? (I've known people who've done just that.) The next-door neighbours may have just installed a gorgeous new kitchen – but are they working three jobs apiece to pay off their giant mortgage?

Stop looking to the people around you to measure your own standard of living. Instead, turn your focus inward. What are the things *you* really care about? What are *your* deepest priorities? What kinds of lifestyle decisions will let *you* sleep soundly at night? On self-reflection, most people realise that building a future with financial security is actually more important to them than 'keeping up appearances' or matching their friends goody for goody.

Remember that 'spending money' and 'having fun' are two different things. In a world where advertising is everywhere, we easily fall into the trap of believing that everything good in life involves *buying* something. It may be a product (the latest electronic toy, the newest fashion statement, the hottest car) or a prepackaged experience (a Greek isles cruise, a night at the coolest dance club, a day at the race track). In reality, there's much truth in the words of the old song: 'The best things in life are free.'

Think about your happiest life memories. Some of them no doubt involve paid-for activities – a family holiday, a wedding, a special Christmas gift – but many are built around virtually cost-free times with people you love – a day on the beach or in your favourite park, an evening of telling ghost stories or watching a great old movie on the telly, an afternoon of playing cards or board games while gossiping with your friends.

When the time is right to launch your personal savings programme, make a plan to rediscover some of the many ways you can have fun without spending a lot of money. Learn an art or a craft; join a club or social group; read that novel you've always meant to read; take up walking, jogging, hiking or cycling; do volunteer work or get involved with local politics. Sometimes we spend too much money simply because we've forgotten how enjoyable it can be to get personally engaged in activities we really care about.

Where to Put Your Savings

Feeling ready to take the plunge and get started with some serious saving? That's great! In the next few chapters, I'll be offering some detailed advice about how to create a long-range investment plan that will help you make the most of your money, specifically with retirement in mind. We'll look at funds, shares, bonds and other investment vehicles you'll want to consider for their long-term growth potential. But in the short term, as you begin to accumulate the first few thousand pounds out of your daily budget, you'll need a place to put the money that will allow it to grow safely and with minimal fuss on your part.

Here's a quick look at the basic savings options you should consider as you launch your retirement savings programme.

A regular savings account. This is the kind of account I recommended earlier in this chapter. It provides for automatic transfers from your current (cheque) account into your savings account. You set the amount to be transferred, and you are free to increase it or decrease it as circumstances change.

Some automatic savings accounts come with restrictions on the number of withdrawals you can make, and some do not allow lump sum deposits to be made outside of the regular monthly transfers. An account that doesn't include such restrictions – especially the restriction on lump sum deposits – is preferable, since you would like to be able to make extra deposits when you receive your annual bonus or any other special windfall payment. The interest paid will vary from one bank or building society to another and from one time to another, so you will want to shop around to find a good deal when you're ready to open your account.

An easy access account. This is the most basic kind of savings account, which allows you to make deposits and withdrawals at any time without any special notice. Interest rates will vary from bank to bank and, because this part of the marketplace is so competitive, rates are as good as and in some cases even better than what you might earn on a limited access account.

A limited access account. Also called a *notice account*, this kind of savings account places restrictions on your ability to withdraw funds. For example, you may be limited to a fixed number of withdrawals during the course of a year, or you may be required to give notice (say, 30 or 60 days) in advance of any withdrawal. If you fail to provide such notice, you will be penalised by forfeiting some of the interest otherwise payable on the account. As I noted earlier, a limited access account can be a good option for the person who needs a little extra encouragement to maintain the sanctity of his or her savings account.

A bond or term account. This is a relatively high-interest account that requires you to tie up a fixed amount of savings for a set period of time, usually one to five years. Once you deposit your funds in such an account, you normally can't make any additional deposits, nor can you withdraw any of your money prior to the so-called *maturity date* without incurring a penalty. This is a good place to 'park' savings you've accumulated and that you know you will not touch, perhaps while you research other investment opportunities (such as shares or funds).

A tax-free account. In chapter 3, I described the tax-saving properties of ISAs. When saving for your retirement, you should certainly take advantage of the cash ISA option to the fullest extent possible (currently limited to £3,600, but rising to £5,100 by 2010 deposited each year). A cash ISA may contain any of the kinds of savings accounts I've described in this section, and the interest you earn accumulates free of income tax. To open a cash ISA, speak to a representative at the bank or building society where you are considering saving and track down the best rates by looking online. The FSA has its own comparison tables at www.moneymadeclear.fsa.gov.uk.

By launching a savings programme and starting to deposit some money into it every month you have taken a huge step towards building the financial security you need for a happy and comfortable retirement. But there is much more you can do to improve your chances of enjoying the retirement of your dreams. In particular, if you devote a little time and energy to learning about investment options beyond the basic savings account, you can increase the rate at which your money will grow and boost the size of your ultimate retirement nest egg. In the next chapter, I'll begin teaching you what you need to know to make this happen.

5. Creating an Investment Plan

Basic Investment Vehicles

As you've seen, the first step in constructing the third leg of your retirement stool is beginning to save. It's also the hardest step. For many people, accepting the need to change their spending patterns and taking concrete actions to get out of debt and start accumulating money is challenging, even painful.

I hope you've managed to take this first step with the help of the advice I offered in the previous chapter. If so, you can begin thinking about the next step in the process: moving up from saving to investing.

What's the difference? It's simple: *saving* is tucking away money in a virtually risk-free account at a bank or building society, where it can grow slowly but predictably over time; *investing* is shifting some of that money into vehicles that are a little more risky but can potentially grow at a faster rate. For most people who are trying to accumulate a significant sum of money for a major goal, such as retirement, it's important to eventually make the leap from saving to investing – perhaps not in the first year after you launch your retirement programme, but soon thereafter.

During a recession when share prices tend to fall – sometimes significantly – you may think it's a bad time to invest in the stock market, especially for your pension. There are two perspectives on this situation. On the positive side, many analysts believe that the current recession presents one of the best buying opportunities in years. Some of the best-known corporations in the UK and the US are selling at amazingly low prices, especially considering their growth opportunities when the economy turns and recovers. So if you are an investor with a long-term time horizon (such as retirement) then buying into these companies now could make sense. However, on the negative side, if you are hoping to buy these shares at the lowest prices, you could, as they say in the markets, be catching a falling knife. This means the shares could drop even more, resulting in your losing money and some of your retirement funds before the market begins to recover. The decision about whether you buy shares now or later comes down to your risk tolerance.

When you are ready to consider investing you'll find there are various choices of investment vehicles – that is, types of investments (also called *securities*). In fact, there are so many ways to invest that even learning all their names can be very daunting. But in this book, I promise to keep it simple (well, as simple as possible). I'll focus on the securities that are suitable to most people – in particular, to people who are *not* financial experts and have no desire to become such.

If you fall into this category, there are just three basic kinds of securities you ought to know about in order to create a retirement investment plan:

- **Shares.** A share is a certificate representing part-ownership in a company. When you buy a share, you are buying a small part of the company and are entitled to a share of its profits. Part of these profits are generally paid to the shareholders annually in the form of *dividends*. In addition, if the revenues and profits of the company increase over time, the value of the company generally increases, and with it the value of the shares, which can then be sold at a profit. This is part of the reason why shares are considered a very attractive investment vehicle

– there are two ways you can hope to profit whenever you invest in shares. ·

- **Bonds.** A bond is basically an IOU. When you buy a bond, you are lending money to a company, a government agency or another institution. The entity that issues the bond (and which therefore is borrowing money from you) promises to pay you a fixed amount of interest at regular intervals over a set period of time (the *term*). It also promises to repay the amount borrowed (the *capital*) on a fixed date, which is known as the *maturity date* of the bond.

- **Unit trusts.** A unit trust is a collection (or *portfolio*) of securities (usually shares or bonds) chosen and managed by a professional – a finance expert with experience, knowledge and judgment about investing. When you invest in a unit trust, you are buying a portion of that portfolio, and you will share in the dividends or interest generated, as well as the increase (or decrease) in value of the portfolio. There are other kinds of pooled investments similar to unit trusts, called *open-ended investment companies* (OEICs), which operate according to slightly different rules and investment trusts (which are different again). For simplicity, in this chapter I'll refer to all pooled investments as unit trusts. [Note: while some books would lump unit trusts together with shares as 'stock market investing', I'm separating them because of their different risk profiles.]

Within these categories there are many variations – numerous kinds of shares, bonds and unit trusts, each designed to cater to a particular type of investor or investment objective. I'll explain some of the variations later. As you'll see, they range widely in their suitability for the average investor. So don't assume that all investments in a single category are similar. The most important rule is: know what you are buying, and learn enough about its characteristics to be certain it's an appropriate investment for you.

There are also many other kinds of investments you'll see touted in adverts or mentioned in the business news. Some are *derivatives* of various kinds, so-called because they involve recombinations of other securities in new forms that *derive* their value from the underlying investments. These derivatives include options, futures, collateralised mortgage obligations (CMOs), and so on. These are complex, generally highly risky and *not* suitable for the average investor.

Rather than investing in securities, some people prefer to use their savings to buy physical objects – antiques, fine art, precious metals, rare books, vintage cars and postage stamps. These things can be fun to buy and pleasant to collect. My weakness is for contemporary art, especially photographs and drawings; I have a collection of pictures that I like to hang on the walls of my home, and some of them have risen in value over time. But collectibles should *not* be used as investment vehicles by the average person. The fact is that most collectors lose more than they gain; the only ones who profit (beside the dealers) are a few collectors with indepth knowledge of the field, personal connections and good luck. Buy art or antiques if you like – but don't bet your retirement on them.

In this book, we'll focus our attention on shares, bonds and unit trusts, which are the investment vehicles of choice for the overwhelming majority of people.

What every Investor Needs to Know about Risk

I've already mentioned the word *risk* a couple of times in this chapter. In fact, I used the concept of risk to differentiate saving (which is practically risk-free) from investing (which always carries some risk). But the meaning of risk in this financial concept is far from obvious, and it bears a bit of explanation.

What is risk? Many definitions have been suggested, but I prefer a simple one: *risk is the possibility of financial loss.* And in the real world, every investment carries with it at least some degree of risk. That is, no matter what investment vehicle you put your money into, there is always at least a small chance that you may lose some or all of your money. But the degree of risk varies greatly from one type of investment to the next. Think of a kind of 'risk ladder', with different securities arranged along it according to the degree of risk they bear.

The risk involved in investing, therefore, runs on a scale from very high to very low, depending largely on the specific investment vehicles you choose. Therefore, one of the basic considerations in developing your own investment plan is to decide *how much risk* you are willing to bear. Having made that decision, you can begin choosing securities that fit the risk profile that is right for you.

The chart on page 98 offers one possible presentation of the risk ladder, from a building society savings account (low risk) to so-called derivative instruments like financial futures (high risk). (Don't worry if some of the terms on this chart are unfamiliar to you now. I'll explain them later.) In general, riskier investments carry greater possibility of financial loss. In addition, they fluctuate in value more greatly. Whereas a low-risk investment tends to rise or fall in value within a narrow range, never getting too high or too low, a high-risk investment may swing in value rather wildly, shooting sky-high one month and falling off the cliff the next. These extreme value fluctuations are part of what makes high-risk investments risky, because there's a chance you may find you have to sell your investment (to fund your retirement, for example) at a time when the value is low.

Our chart of the risk ladder contains two horizontal lines, which divide the ladder into three segments. The horizontal line near the bottom of the risk ladder chart represents what might be called the investment threshold: below the line are securities that are practically risk-free and therefore suitable for savings, while the vehicles above the line all carry significant risk and therefore should be considered as suitable for investing. The horizontal line near the top separates very high-risk investments (often described as *speculative*) from those that carry moderate risks.

Depending on your personal risk tolerance, you may choose to spend most of your time towards the bottom of the ladder, where risks are lower, or venture more boldly up the ladder with at least a portion of your money. But you should certainly concentrate on the middle section of the ladder, among the investment vehicles I've labelled as having moderate risk. These are the choices most investors should consider.

The Risk Ladder

Highest Risk	Derivatives – futures, options, CMOs etc
	Collectibles – art, antiques, gold, stamps etc
Moderate Risk	Small-cap shares
	Mid-cap shares
	Blue chip (large-cap) shares
	Investment trusts
	Unit trusts invested in shares
	Corporate bonds
	Unit trusts invested in bonds
Lowest Risk	Gilts (UK government bonds)
	Savings accounts (bank or building society)
	National Savings
	Cash ISA

At this point, you may be wondering, 'Why on earth would I want to choose investment vehicles that carry risk? Isn't risk a *bad* thing that I should avoid at all costs?' Actually, accepting a certain degree of risk is a good idea for most investors. The reason is that – as centuries of financial history have demonstrated – a reasonable amount of risk brings with it the likelihood of greater financial reward.

Here is the paradox of risk: *in general, the greater the risk you are willing to undertake, the greater the potential gains you may enjoy.* In other words, for most investments, the size of the potential profit is closely related to the size of the potential losses.

The paradox of risk means that an investment strategy designed to reduce risk as much as possible is likely to yield growth that is steady but slow. By contrast, a very risky strategy – one that accepts high risk in hopes of huge profits – could produce results ranging from spectacularly good to horrendously bad, depending on your timing, your cleverness and your luck.

For most investors, the best choice is a strategy that falls somewhere between these two extremes – accepting a modest amount of risk in exchange for relatively robust growth. But deciding exactly where on the risk ladder you want to live – and finding investments that will take you there – takes a bit of thought and information.

How much Risk Is Right for You?

The answer to this question depends in part on your psychology. Any investment mix that would make it hard for you to sleep at night is wrong for you. This means that knowing yourself and recognising how risk-averse or risk-tolerant you are is important in planning your investment approach.

One way of determining your personal attitude towards

investment risk is to think about your comfort level with other forms of risk. When you and your friends visit an amusement park, do you rush to ride the tallest, fastest and scariest roller coaster – or do you prefer more sedate and down-to-earth attractions? When choosing a course of study at college, did you pick one that matched a personal passion, regardless of whether it might lead to a lucrative career – or did you gravitate towards a field that promised steady work and a lifetime of financial security? When deciding between two job offers, would you be inclined to favour one with a small, fast-growing and exciting company in a new and rapidly-changing industry – or would you be more comfortable with a job at a large, established and well-known company in a solid, slow-moving field? The answers to questions like these can help you discern whether your personality is more risk-friendly or risk-avoiding.

If you aren't sure how you feel about investment risk, I suggest you start investing with lower-risk vehicles. (I'll explain how to find these in a moment.) As you gain experience, knowledge and self-confidence, you can always choose to move some of your money into higher-risk investments if you want.

However, your choices in regard to investment risk shouldn't be determined solely by your personality. They should also depend in part on your age and your financial objectives. Here's why.

Ideally, you should adjust your risk tolerance depending on the time frame of your main investment goals. Suppose you are investing mainly for a short-term goal – a deposit on a home purchase, a new car, a once-in-a-lifetime holiday, or a home renovation – which you expect to reach within one to five years. In that case, it makes sense to avoid high-risk vehicles, since if you suffer a loss you'll have little time in which to make it back.

By contrast, suppose you are investing mainly for a long-term goal – such as your retirement 30 years in the future. In that case, you can afford to incur somewhat greater risk. Why? Because, although riskier investment vehicles fluctuate more in value, over time most investment vehicles will gradually increase in value. For example, if you invest in shares, even if the stock market goes through a down period, the chances are good that the market will bounce back and rise again before your retirement rolls around.

For the same reason, many investors like to shift their investment strategy over time, as dictated by the changing time frame of their personal financial goals. I'll discuss this approach later, when I talk about the important investment technique known as *asset allocation*.

Now, let's take a closer look at the three basic kinds of investment vehicle you should consider for your personal retirement account. In particular, I'll give you some ideas about the risk characteristics of each type of investment, so you can begin to think about which options might work best for your retirement plan.

Basic Facts about Shares

As I've explained, shares represent partial ownership of a company. They are issued by companies as a way of raising money, and they are subsequently traded among investors on stock exchanges, which are marketplaces established for the purpose. Share prices rise and fall along with the company's financial prospects, and a large part of the art of investing in shares lies in learning how to spot companies that are ready to expand and become more profitable. The shares of such companies will usually respond by rising in value, to the benefit of the investors who own them.

This explains why the business news programmes on the radio and TV are generally filled with stories about the good or bad fortunes of individual companies – which firms are enjoying record sales, which are suffering declines in profits and which are developing new goods or services that are likely to attract eager buyers. These stories are important for investors who are looking for ideas about which company shares to buy.

Generally speaking, shares carry the highest risk of any investment vehicle that the average investor should consider. This makes sense – after all, it's hard to predict what the future will bring for any particular company whose shares you might buy. But this higher risk is coupled with the possibility of a relatively high return. Over the past 40 years, UK shares have averaged an annual investment yield of over 12 per cent. (In other words, if you'd invested your money in shares over this entire period of time, the average growth of your money would have been over 12 per cent per year.) Compare this with an almost risk-free savings account, which (as of early 2009) was producing growth of between 6 and 6.5 per cent per year. It's obvious that well-chosen shares can be an attractive investment that will give your money a good chance to grow at a great rate over a period of years.

When you own shares in a company, you are entitled to some of the company's profits, which are paid out in the form of dividends. Some companies pay out a significant amount of their profits to the investors, which means that dividend payments are high. Others invest most of their profits in future growth, perhaps buying new equipment or expanding into new marketplaces. These companies pay smaller dividends or none at all. However, this doesn't mean that such companies are necessarily bad investments. Investors often buy such shares in the hope that the market price will increase as the company grows.

If retirement is relatively far away for you (say, more than ten years in the future), you will probably want to invest your retirement money mainly in shares of companies that focus on the long-term increase in value (often called *capital growth* shares). By contrast, as retirement nears, you may prefer to invest in high-dividend shares (often called *income* or *high-yielding* shares). Income shares are especially appropriate *after* retirement, since the dividend payments they generate periodically may help support your lifestyle.

When you decide to buy shares, you'll need the help of a *stockbroker.* This is an individual or company authorised to trade shares on an exchange. The broker is paid a fee, called a *commission,* for this service. Some brokers do nothing more than carry out customers' orders to buy or sell shares. These are called *execution-only* brokers. Others also provide investment ideas and financial guidance. These are called *advisory* brokers. Advisory brokers generally charge higher fees than execution-only brokers.

Opening a brokerage account is a fairly simple and easy process. You'll have to fill out a form that asks basic questions about your financial status and the level of investment risk you're prepared to assume. This information will help the broker avoid recommending investments that are unsuitable for you. But remember! The main responsibility for picking investments you can live with is yours and yours alone.

Choosing shares by company size. There are almost as many kinds of shares as there are companies. One of the important breakdowns to be aware of is based on company size. The three broad categories are:

- **Large-caps or blue chips.** These are shares of large, well-established companies in major industry sectors that generally have a track record of increasing revenues and profits. (They're often called blue chips because these are the highest-value chips used in gambling casinos.) Blue-chip stocks make relatively safe investments that are unlikely either to rise or to fall precipitously. But when major changes sweep the economy, even blue-chip companies may collapse. So don't assume that blue-chip stocks are risk-free. Like all shares, they carry some risk.

- **Mid-caps.** These are shares in medium-sized companies, so-called because their market capitalisation – that is, the total value of all the company's ordinary shares on the market – is in the middle range. Mid-cap stocks tend to be somewhat more risky than blue chips; share prices are likely to rise and fall more quickly and unpredictably. However, at any given time, much of the nation's (and the world's) economic growth is concentrated in strong mid-cap companies.
- **Small-caps.** These are shares in small companies. They tend to be relatively risky investments, since small companies are often newer, sometimes based on unknown or experimental products, technologies or markets, and subject to rapid swings in value, both up and down. Some of the great investment success stories involve small-caps that grow to become great companies, creating millionaire investors along the way. But be cautious! More people who invest in small-caps lose than gain.

As you can see, the spectrum of stock-issuing companies from large to small generally corresponds to the degree of risk (and the growth potential) offered.

We haven't even mentioned the riskiest category of stocks – the very small, so-called *microcaps*. (This category overlaps with another category, known as *penny stocks*, which get their name from the fact that their per-share price is very low, often under one pound.)

Microcaps and penny stocks are *not* a smart investment for most people, especially for novices. Too often people want to invest in something cheap, assuming it's good value. This leads them to invest in a company that is small and often new. But low price isn't the key – the quality of the company is. Most inexpensive shares (like most small, new companies) are quite speculative. A few of the companies that issue such shares will become very profitable and successful, but most will not. Thus, buying cheap stocks is a little like buying lottery tickets: there's the chance of a great payoff, but most people will lose their money and have nothing at all to show for it.

In order to minimise their risk, many new investors feel most comfortable starting off with blue-chip shares. The leading UK blue chips belong to an index known as the FTSE 100 (pronounced 'footsie' and an abbreviation for Financial Times Stock Exchange Index). This is a collection of companies representing Britain's top 100 companies. Their share prices, combined according to a complex formula, go to make up the FTSE 100 Index, whose value is reported on the news and in the financial pages as a convenient way of measuring the progress of big business in the UK. (When the newsreader reports that 'The FTSE 100 was up today', that's a shorthand way of saying that the financial news was favourable for large companies in Britain.) Some of the familiar company names included in the FTSE 100 are BT, Vodafone, BP, GlaxoSmithKline, Unilever, Tesco, Sainsbury's, Associated British Foods, Scottish & Newcastle and ICI.

Choosing shares by market sector. People also break down the stock market in terms of *sectors* – that is, industries. To give you a feeling for how companies can be grouped in sectors, here's a sampling of some of the sectors into which the FTSE companies are divided:

- Electronic and electrical equipment
- Steel and other metals
- Information technology hardware
- Mining
- Oil and gas
- Personal care and household products
- Life assurance

- Aerospace and defence
- Food and drug retailers

As you can imagine, different sectors tend to react differently to varying economic conditions. In times of military crisis, the defence sector benefits. When devastating hurricanes or earthquakes strike, property insurance firms suffer. When increased demand for energy drives the price of crude oil higher, oil and gas firms thrive.

When considering a share purchase, it makes sense to evaluate both the industry sector and the individual company. First, consider the overall strength of the sector and the likelihood that it will grow in sales and profits in the coming years. Then consider the individual company. How does it compare to other companies in the sector? Is it one of the best managed, most profitable and fastest growing companies in the sector? If so, it stands a good chance of out-performing the rest of the sector.

Learning more about shares. As you can see, investing in shares can be complicated. The best share investors take the time to learn about industry sectors, company histories, economic trends and corporate strategies, hoping to identify tomorrow's hot growth company before others do. For many people – perhaps most – this is an onerous task they'd rather not be saddled with. But for some, it's a fascinating pastime that can also be quite lucrative.

If you get bitten by the share investing bug, there are several excellent sources of information on companies and the shares they offer. One is *Company Refs* (www.companyrefs.com) a monthly book with a page of detailed data on each company covered. Or you can call your broker and ask him or her to send you the latest analyst's report on a company you're interested in.

Basic Facts about Bonds

As I've explained, a bond is an IOU. When you buy a bond, you are lending money to a company or a government agency, which promises to repay the loan, with interest, over a specific period of time, known as the term. Bonds issued by companies are known as *corporate bonds*; bonds issued by the British government are often called *gilts*.

As an investment, bonds are generally considered lower-risk than shares. There are several reasons for this. For one thing, the amount of income you'll enjoy from your bond is spelled out in advance, in the form of the fixed rate of interest promised by the bond issuer. (This rate is sometimes referred to as the *coupon*.) Bond issuers have to make these payments when they are due; if they miss a payment, they are said to be in default.

Another reason bonds are considered relatively low-risk is that when a company goes bankrupt and its assets are sold off, the law generally provides that bondholders should be paid before shareholders. Hopefully bankruptcy will never strike any company you invest in, but if it does you will be better off as a bondholder, since ordinary shareholders come last in line among those to be paid off and typically get nothing.

Of course, bonds are not completely risk-free – as I've repeatedly stressed in this chapter, no investment is. As I've mentioned, companies do go bankrupt, and sometimes the bondholders are left high and dry, or paid off just a fraction of their investment money. Even governments occasionally default on their debts – as Russia did in 1998. But most nations will do everything possible to avoid default, since it makes it difficult and costly for them to borrow additional money for years to come. Obviously the British government is one of the most stable and secure in the world, and the risk of default on UK-issued bonds is very, very small.

Bonds also carry other, more subtle forms of risk. After their issuance, bonds can be bought and sold on an exchange or other trading market (generally through a broker or dealer, like shares). The price of a bond on this *aftermarket* will vary from time to time, based mainly on changes in interest rates. Here's how this works. Suppose you buy a bond that is paying interest at an annual rate of 5.5 per cent. If interest rates rise, so that comparable bonds are paying, say, 6.5 per cent, your coupon will become less desirable to other investors. As a result, the selling price of your bond will fall. On the other hand, if interest rates fall to, say, 4.5 per cent, your 5.5 per cent coupon will look very attractive, and the price of your bond will rise. Thus, the value of your bond is subject to interest rate risk.

Another, even more subtle, form of risk affecting bonds is *inflation risk*. As we discussed in chapter 2, inflation is the tendency of prices to increase over time. Thanks to inflation, the value of money gradually shrinks. Normally, this is a very slow process. But when inflation accelerates, the value of a rate of interest that seemed fair at the time a bond was issued will be eroded as the buying power of the pound shrinks. If you hold a bond with a 4 per cent coupon, and inflation rises to 6 per cent annually, your investment will actually be *losing* value every year, despite the interest payments you are receiving. When the bond principal is repaid, you'll be able to buy fewer groceries and other products than you would have when you initially invested the money.

Of course, all risks work both ways. Whenever you take on the possibility of losing money, you also take on the possibility of profit. This applies to bonds. Suppose you happen to buy a bond with a high coupon during a time of high inflation. If and when the inflation rate falls, the income generated by your bond will become even more valuable. You may end up with income of, say, 10 per cent per year in a world where most people must be content with 6 per cent. That's not quite as nice as owning a money tree, but it's close!

As this example suggests, bond investors need to pay attention to overall economic conditions. There are times when bonds make a great investment, and other times when most smart investors avoid them. If you're thinking about putting some of your retirement money into bonds – not a bad idea for most investors – begin paying attention to the news about economic trends and interest-rate fluctuations, and note how this affects bond values. Over time, this will help you develop a feeling for how bond returns are likely to move.

Types of bonds. Just as there are many kinds of shares with differing degrees of risk (and potential reward), there are various kinds of bonds. Although as a generalisation it's correct to say that bonds carry lower risk than shares, there are exceptions at both ends of the spectrum. Some of the most important types of bonds are:

- **Gilts (government bonds).** As I've mentioned, these are bonds issued by the British government, considered extremely safe as investments. Every gilt has a so-called *par value* of £100. This is the amount you'll receive as a repayment if you hold the bond to maturity (that is, throughout its term). In addition, of course, you'll receive regular interest payments as long as you hold the bond. Most gilts have terms of five, ten or 15 years, and they can be purchased through a stockbroker, or from Computershare (which has taken over selling gilts from the Bank of England) at www.computershare.com or 0870 703 0143.

- **Corporate bonds.** These are issued by companies as a way of raising funds. The risk you assume when you buy a corporate bond depends on the financial strength of the company that issued it. Bonds issued by large, profitable, long-established businesses in stable industries can be almost as safe as government bonds, while bonds issued by small, new firms may be quite risky. The most risky corporate bonds are sometimes called *junk bonds* or *high-yield bonds*. (For obvious reasons, the bond salespeople prefer the latter term!) Most investors – especially novices – should steer clear of the junk bond market.

The interest rate paid by a particular company or issuer's bonds will usually vary directly with the degree of risk entailed. Bonds issued by blue-chip firms pay relatively low interest rates; risky junk bonds promise high interest payments – but of course there's the chance the company may go belly-up, and you may receive nothing at all.

Why own bonds? There are several good reasons why an investor planning his or her retirement might want to own bonds. The most important are:

- **To generate low-risk income.** An investor who is mainly interested in producing a reliable, steady stream of current income (rather than in building a nest egg for the future through growth) will probably want to put a significant part of his or her portfolio into bonds. Many retirees use government bonds or low-risk corporate bonds for this purpose. (As I mentioned earlier, high-dividend shares can play a similar role in your investment portfolio.)
- **To balance the risk involved in owning shares.** Generally speaking, shares grow in value along with the companies they represent. Therefore, during hard times, when the national or world economy (or large sectors of the economy) fail to grow, shares are apt to stagnate or fall in value. By contrast, bond values often increase at such times. Therefore, you may want to put some of your investment money into bonds to balance, or *hedge*, the risk in your share portfolio.

One easy way of getting started in bond investing is by buying shares in a unit trust that specialises in bonds. I'll explain how this works in the next section.

Basic Facts about Unit Trusts – the Novice Investor's Best Friend

Throughout this chapter, I've emphasised the notion that higher risk and higher rates of growth usually go together. To make more money on your investments, you usually must accept a higher level of risk, which means a greater chance that you could lose some or all of your money. It's the financial equivalent of the truth every athlete-in-training knows: 'No pain, no gain'.

But what if you could achieve a relatively high rate of growth while carrying a relatively lower level of risk? That would be the best of both worlds, wouldn't it?

Beware of cold calls by high pressure 'stockbrokers' or Internet scam artists promising this kind of 'miracle investment'. Practically always, such something-for-nothing schemes are phoney deals designed to take your money and give you nothing in return. But there is one proven technique for reducing risk while maintaining relatively high investment growth. It's known as *diversification*.

Diversification is a financial strategy that involves investing in shares or bonds issued by companies from several different sectors, including sectors that tend to move in opposite directions. When you diversify, you reduce your risk of losing money based on bad news affecting one or a few investments. At the same time, you retain most of the potential for gains that shares and bonds can offer.

For example, if some of your money is invested in shares of consumer products companies (like retailers and food suppliers), a diversification strategy might lead you to invest a separate sum in shares of industrial companies (like aerospace manufacturers and information technology firms). These sectors are so different in their relation to the overall economy that, when one sector falls, chances are good that the other will rise or stay the same, minimising your chance of suffering a catastrophic loss.

Many studies conducted over decades have confirmed that diversification can improve the overall performance of an investment portfolio significantly. But there's only one problem: it generally takes at least ten to 12 different investments to create a truly diversified portfolio. And building such a portfolio is tough for many individual investors. For one thing, they may not have enough money in their retirement plans to own reasonable quantities of the many different shares or bonds needed. For another, it requires a lot of time and energy to research, buy, monitor and periodically replace holdings in such a large, complex portfolio. Most people with day jobs just don't want to bother.

Here is where the unit trust shows another important value as an investment vehicle. As I explained earlier, a unit trust is a pooled investment – a portfolio of shares or bonds selected and managed by a professional investor using funds pooled from thousands of individual investors. When you invest in a unit trust, you buy a *unit* of the fund. As the value of all the shares in the trust portfolio rises (or falls), so does the value of each unit you own. As an investor in the unit trust, you can elect to have dividends earned by the shares in the portfolio either paid out to you or reinvested in the fund. If you choose the latter, the total value of the portfolio increases, as does the number of units you own.

For most people, a unit trust is an excellent first investment choice. A unit trust is easy to buy directly from the company that manages it, and you can start investing for a modest sum. You can even sign up for a savings scheme by which £20 or £50 per month is automatically invested in the unit trust of your choice. This will enable you to take advantage of pound-cost averaging. By putting in small amounts of money at regular intervals, your money will buy more shares when prices are low and fewer when prices are high. Over time the result is that the average cost per share ends up being lower than the average price per share for the same period.

Best of all, a unit trust offers the average investor a quick and easy way of achieving diversification, thereby reducing the degree of exposure to stock-specific risk. When a particular company suffers a downturn, chances are good that other stocks owned by your unit trust may be moving up, thus making up for some of the decline. (Of course, when the entire stock market is in the tank, many unit trusts will go downhill as well.)

A unit trust also generally has the advantage of professional management. The investment managers who buy and sell shares or bonds on behalf of unit trusts spend all their time evaluating specific companies and their management, studying the economic environment, and developing strategies they hope will produce profits for their investors. Although like anyone else they are fallible, they are better informed than the average beginning investor.

Naturally, the managers of the unit trust expect to be compensated for their work on your behalf. They are paid in two basic ways. The first is through an initial charge when you buy into the unit trust, which averages 5 per cent of the amount you invest. A good discount stockbroker can cut this charge significantly. The second is through an annual charge, which is deducted from the overall value of the fund. The annual charge averages between 1 and 1.5 per cent of the fund's value. It's worth considering these charges when deciding on a unit trust investment. Other things being equal, a unit trust that charges lower fees may be a more profitable long-term investment.

Types of unit trusts. There are almost 1,800 different unit trusts to choose from in the UK. Each is managed by a different individual or team, and each operates according to a slightly different investment philosophy. However, the many types of trusts tend to fall into several general categories. What follows is a list of the most popular types of trusts, with some indication of the kind of investor who ought to consider each.

- **Index-tracker funds** are designed to follow the performance of a popular stock market index, such as the FTSE 100. The managers of a tracker fund either buy shares in all the companies that make up the index or buy shares in a representative sampling of those companies. For various reasons, tracker funds have generally out-performed most other unit trusts, and because they usually have relatively low charges they are an attractive option for most retirement investors.
- **Equity income funds** focus on companies that pay high dividends. These trusts are a good choice for investors who seek a low-risk investment that offers relatively high current income (though with limited long-term growth prospects). Thus, retirees or those who are approaching retirement age often favour equity income funds in their investment portfolios.
- **Capital growth funds** invest in companies whose share prices are expected to increase substantially. Investors with long time horizons – say, those who are at least ten years or more away from retirement – should consider investing in capital growth funds.
- **Small-cap funds** invest in smaller companies that are considered to have strong growth prospects. Since the long-term performance of companies in this category is very hard to predict, these trusts are relatively risky. In a bad year, you could lose 20, 30 or even 50 per cent of your total investment in a small-cap fund. But in a good year,

you could double your money. If you are young (at least 20 years from retirement) and risk-tolerant, you may want to invest a portion of your retirement money in a small-cap fund, but if you do, be prepared for a rocky ride.

- **Global funds** (also known as *world funds*) invest in foreign shares and shares of UK companies that do significant business overseas. Depending on the mix of countries, regions and industries selected by the trust manager, global funds can be rather risky. During the Asian financial crisis of the mid-1990s, for instance, many global funds suffered badly. But because the economies of the emerging world (Latin America, Asia and the former Iron Curtain countries) were growing faster than those of Europe and North America, well-managed global funds had relatively strong long-term growth prospects for several years. Those who are a decade or more away from retirement may want to consider adding a global fund to their investments.

- **International funds** invest solely outside the UK. They have many of the same characteristics as global funds but are generally even more risky. The same is true of regional funds, which invest in shares of companies from a particular region of the world – Asia, the former Soviet bloc or Latin America, for example. Younger, more risk-tolerant investors with a strong feeling about the economic prospects of the developing world may consider such funds.

- **Sector funds** invest in specific industries. These funds perform as well or as poorly as the industries they focus on. During the high-tech boom of the late 1990s, high-tech funds performed spectacularly; since the high-tech bust of 2000, most of those gains have evaporated. The same is true of banks and financial services companies in 2008–09. If you are a decade or more away from retirement, and if you feel strongly that a particular industry (whether it's pharmaceuticals, entertainment, health care or consumer goods) is due for a period of rapid growth, consider using a portion of your retirement account to buy shares in an appropriate sector fund.

- **Bond funds** invest in bonds rather than shares. Some concentrate on government bonds (gilts), others on corporate bonds. Buying bond funds can be a convenient, low-risk way of including some bonds in your investment portfolio. Since bonds and shares generally move in opposite directions, this can help to balance some of the risk involved in owning shares. As I'll discuss later in this chapter, most investors should make bonds part of their retirement portfolio.

- **Ethical funds** (also known as *socially responsible funds*) invest in shares of companies that meet specified moral criteria. For example, some ethical funds avoid companies that make military equipment, tobacco products or alcoholic beverages; others choose companies with stellar environmental records or a strong track record of hiring and promoting women and minority group members. Many ethical funds have performed well over time, so consider investing in such a fund if you have strong moral principles you'd like to back up with your money.

This is just a sampling of the kinds of trusts currently available. New trust types are emerging all the time, limited only by the ingenuity of fund managers (and of the marketing arms of the financial firms). Take some time to read about the various fund types and try to compare your investment interests and objectives with those of the funds you're considering. When you find a good match, you may want to make a purchase. Also keep in mind that unit trusts and investment trusts can be held in tax-efficient vehicles such as ISAs or SIPPs.

Evaluating performance. Many investors try to select a unit trust on the basis of past performance. That is, they look at the growth of the value of the trust over the past one, three or five years and use this to extrapolate future performance. The assumption is that the fund that has earned the greatest profits for investors in the recent past is likely to do the same in the future.

It's certainly worthwhile to consider past performance when evaluating a unit trust. (And managers whose funds have performed well will certainly encourage you to do so!) History shows that a few investment managers have been able to outperform their competitors over time, earning significantly better returns for their clients.

However, it's easy to give past performance more weight than it deserves. This is true for several reasons:

- Short-term performance is partly a matter of luck, good or bad. Quite often the fund at the top of its category in a given year does no better than middling or even below-average in the following year, while last year's low-rated fund rises to the top of the heap.
- Fund managers switch jobs from time to time. The fund that earned huge profits last year may be headed by an entirely different team this year, making past performance that much harder to replicate.
- Funds often rise or fall based on unpredictable or cyclic economic factors. Money managers who looked like geniuses when the dot-com shares were booming suddenly looked like imbeciles when the bottom fell out of that marketplace. In truth, they were neither geniuses nor imbeciles – they just happened to be in the right place one year and in the wrong place the next.

A good source of information on unit trusts is www.morningstar. co.uk or www.trustnet.com. Morningstar and Trustnet rate unit trusts by risk and track their long-term results. They're an excellent source of basic data that can be very helpful in selecting one or two trusts to get started with.

Asset Allocation

As your retirement investment portfolio grows in value (and complexity) you'll need to consider another component of your investment strategy. *Asset allocation* is the art of deciding how to divide your portfolio among various kinds of investment holdings so as to produce a risk-reward pattern that makes sense for you.

First, recall a couple of basic facts about risk:

- Risk and potential reward tend to vary together. The greater the risk you undertake, the greater the potential for profit.
- The amount of risk you should assume depends partly on your own psychology – how comfortable you are with the possibility of loss.
- It should also depend partly on your financial goals and especially on their time frame. When you are close to retirement, most of your money should be invested in less risky vehicles; when you are further away from your retirement goal, more of your money may be invested in more risky vehicles.

Based on these principles, investment experts have developed a number of formulas for asset allocation. These formulas are designed to combine different kinds of investments into a single portfolio that matches a particular investment style and philosophy. In general, these formulas involve blends of two or three kinds of holdings:

- Shares, including unit trusts that own shares
- Bonds, including unit trusts that own bonds
- Cash, including savings accounts with banks or building societies and cash ISAs

One traditional asset-allocation model is known as the *age-adjusted mix*. This is a formula designed to move from relatively risky to fairly conservative over time. The formula is:

100 – your age = percentage in stocks

The remainder would be allocated to bonds and cash. Thus, when you are 30 years old this model would allocate 70 per cent of your portfolio to stocks (30 per cent to bonds). When you are 65, and ready to retire, this model would allocate 35 per cent of your portfolio to stocks (65 per cent to bonds and cash).

Many people have enjoyed success over the past several decades investing in accordance with the age-adjusted mix. However, with more people living longer after retirement, traditional approaches to asset allocation are being reconsidered. If you have a good chance of living past age 80, and perhaps well into your 90s (as many people today do), there's a greater danger than ever that you could outlive your money.

This means that it's important to keep your money invested in growing assets later in the game than in the past. Shifting heavily into low-risk, low-growth, income-producing investments such as government bonds on retirement may no longer be a viable strategy. Instead, many retirees are opting to keep a larger portion of their investments in shares, so that their nest egg can continue to grow even after age 65.

Research by Ibbotson Associates based on returns from the past 80 years shows that a person with a nest egg of $1.2 million (US) who has 75 per cent of those assets invested in bonds can expect to withdraw only $35,000 per year from the account without touching capital. By contrast, if the same nest egg were invested 75 per cent in stocks, the withdrawal amount would be $80,000 per year.

Of course, there's no guarantee that future returns will follow the same pattern as those in the past. But the same principle holds: stocks, while riskier, also generate higher returns. And today's longer-lived seniors will need those higher returns to support themselves in style through a protracted retirement. So the old asset allocation rules may need some modification.

One way some people are modifying the old rules is by changing the magic number in the age-adjusted mix formula from 100 to 110.

110 – your age = percentage in stocks

According to this new formula, when you are 30 years old, this model would allocate 80 per cent of your portfolio to stocks (20 per cent to bonds and cash). At the retirement age of 65, this model would allocate 45 per cent of your portfolio to stocks (55 per cent to bonds and cash). This change obviously increases the portion of your money in stocks, which, while risky, should help generate the growth and income you'll need to support today's longer retirement period.

No single formula will work for everyone, however. The best thing you can do at every age is to monitor your retirement investments periodically and make sure that they are growing fast enough to achieve the goals you've selected for yourself. If they are, you can stay the course, shifting to less aggressive, safer investments slowly over time. If they aren't, consider shifting to a more aggressive, growth-oriented mix of investments. Like a sailor watching the winds and adjusting the sails as needed to stay on course, you can modify your investments

as circumstances change without ever losing sight of your ultimate goal – a safe and enjoyable retirement lifestyle. I'll provide
more detailed guidance on monitoring and management of your
investments over time later in this book.

6. Whom Do You Trust?

Continuing Your Financial Education

If you've read this book from page one, you've noticed a number of references to today's challenging financial climate. In some ways, individuals now bear more responsibility for their own financial futures than ever before. Most people today change jobs more frequently than in the past, so their occupational pensions are more complex and, in some cases, less reliable. Most people can expect to live longer after retirement, placing greater stress on their personal savings. And most also hope for a more active, affluent lifestyle than past generations of retirees enjoyed, making the challenge of saving for retirement even greater.

But the news isn't all bad. We're also lucky to be living in a time when sound, easy-to-understand money advice is more widely available than ever before. This book, of course, is an example. And there are many other sources you can turn to as you continue your financial education. This is important, because you bear the ultimate responsibility for your long-term economic security. In our rapidly-changing economic world, this means that lifetime financial learning is a requirement, not an option.

Here are some of the sources of financial information that you should become familiar with:

- The money pages or personal finance sections in newspapers and related websites

- Magazines that focus on financial and investment topics
- TV and radio programmes (and their websites) and news coverage related to financial markets and economic developments
- Books on personal finance
- Investment and money management websites on the Internet
- Financial seminars, workshops and courses
- Government agencies
- Trade associations and financial services firms
- Personal financial and investment advisers

Of course, not all of these sources are equally reliable. Consider the Internet. Information spreads faster and easier on the Internet than anywhere else. And because no one edits or controls much of its content, everyone is free to contribute ideas. Search on the Net for information on a topic like 'retirement planning' or 'stakeholder pensions' and you'll find thousands of websites offering information. Unfortunately, not all will be helpful. Some will contain scanty information; others will offer material that is dated, incomplete or inaccurate; and many will be biased because they are compiled by individuals or organisations that are selling something and therefore want to push a particular point of view that may *not* be best for you.

When you're trying to separate the reliable from the treacherous in today's flood of financial information, start by using the same sort of common sense and scepticism you'd apply to a television advert or a door-to-door salesperson. Always consider *who will benefit* from any advice you read or hear. A person or company with an interest in selling a particular financial product or service has a huge incentive to slant the information they present – not necessarily by lying but by playing down or ignoring the risks and over-emphasising the potential benefits. (And there *are* firms and individuals who don't boggle at committing out-and-out fraud.)

Part of evaluating any financial information source is considering its reputation, background and history. Read as widely as you can, comparing the recommendations from various sources. An investment strategy touted only by one or two obscure firms ought to be examined with extreme scepticism, while a strategy that's been widely reported, tested by independent journalists and industry experts, and used with success for years by many individuals may be worth considering for your own portfolio.

So there's a lot you can do to advance your own money knowledge, enabling you to make many money decisions on your own. But for many people, there comes a point when soliciting professional advice is important – when your personal finances are a bit too complicated to handle on your own. I'll spend the rest of this chapter explaining how to go about finding the most reliable sources of professional financial help and how to work with them for your benefit.

When Professional Help Is Needed

For most people, the earliest, simplest stages of developing a personal financial plan – including a savings programme for retirement – can be handled independently. You probably don't need an adviser if you are looking for a straightforward stakeholder pension; you just need to compare the terms and conditions of four to six different providers and make your choice.

But you may need professional advice or services to help you with more complex or advanced forms of financial planning. For example, you should consider engaging a professional financial adviser if:

• Your finances are disorganised and you need to be able
  to understand what you have and how you can budget.

(If you have serious debt problems, go to a debt advice charity such as Citizens Advice instead).

- You're in the market for life insurance, a private pension plan, a savings plan or an annuity, and are unsure which product will best suit your needs.
- You need help in developing a savings and investment programme for goals like retirement, having tried and failed to create a plan on your own.
- You want to begin investing in unit trusts, shares or bonds, and feel uncertain about how to get started.
- You already own a number of pension plans, unit trusts, annuities or other investments and don't know whether they add up to a coherent and appropriate investment strategy.
- You are facing a major change in your life situation (marriage, divorce, retirement, selling off a business) and aren't sure how to adjust your finances accordingly.
- You've built up a large estate and are concerned about reducing the inheritance tax liability your heirs will face.

If one or more of these circumstances fits you, then the time may have come when your personal finances are a bit too complicated for you to handle on your own.

Finding and Working with a Financial Adviser

Of course, it's not enough to recognise that you may need financial help. It's equally important to decide what *kind* of help you need and what sort of professional is best equipped to provide it. Here's a brief rundown of the main types of financial advisers, with some guidelines as to what kind of help you can expect from each one. In the Retail Distribution Review (RDR) published in November 2008, the types of financial advisors were reduced to two: independent advice and sales advice. Those in the independent advice group cover the whole of the market, are fee based, and have higher qualifications. All other types of financial advisors are categorised as sales advisors. I will describe the current situation as the charges are not due to be introduced before 2012.

Independent Financial Advisers (IFAs). The job of an IFA is to provide financial advice on investments and other money matters based on your personal status, current assets and long-range goals. The IFA may be paid a flat fee or an hourly fee, or he may receive all or part of his compensation from commissions based on sales of financial products he recommends to clients – for example, insurance policies, annuities, unit trusts and so on. (Note: throughout this chapter, I'll use the pronouns 'he' and 'him' to refer to a financial adviser. This is purely for simplicity; of course, there are many talented women working in financial services, and I don't mean to slight or ignore them.)

IFAs have to offer you the chance of paying by fee or commission (otherwise they have to call themselves 'financial advisers' not independent financial advisers). Think carefully about how you pay. You might think that paying a commission is more attractive (as you don't have to pay out money upfront), but you won't know whether your IFA's advice was influenced by the commission. Also some IFAs will offset their fees against commission and rebate the rest into your policy, so you get the best of both worlds.

The method of payment can be an important factor in deciding how to evaluate his advice. If you pay your IFA a fee you can be reasonably certain he will provide unbiased investment suggestions. Since he is being paid directly by you for his time and expertise, rather than being paid based on sales of securities, he has no special incentive to recommend a particular type of investment. (Of course, that doesn't mean his suggestions will always be right for you.)

By contrast, if you pay your IFA by commission he may tend

to offer advice that favours investment products on which greater commissions are paid. It's not necessarily that the IFA is consciously trying to take advantage of you. However, it's human nature for a salesperson to feel more enthusiastic about products that offer him greater financial rewards. IFAs vary widely in their knowledge, experience and interests. Not all are equally knowledgeable about every financial field. Be sure to select an IFA with experience working with clients like you, as well as knowledge of the specific financial topics you are most urgently interested in. For example, if you are interested in getting started in the stock market, seek out an IFA with detailed knowledge of shares and other securities, as well as experience in helping clients who are similar to you in income, age and risk tolerance. Seek out IFAs with qualifications such as a diploma from the Personal Finance Society, or, even better, who have qualified as a Certified Financial Planner.

Tied agents. Tied agents are financial salespeople who represent one financial firm and its products. For example, some insurance companies, banks, and building societies employ tied agents to promote their products. Many people cynically apply the following saying to the product offerings of tied agents: 'If the only tool you have is a hammer, everything looks like a nail.' The reality is quite different. Most tied agents sell a whole range of financial products, but only from one company.

Multi-tied agents. As the name suggests, multi-tied agents normally sell products from one of half a dozen or so companies. They are therefore a hybrid of an independent agent and a tied agent. Multi-tied agents may work at banks that have linked up with pension and investments providers, mainly because their own products offer such poor value. Multi-tied advisers may be paid a relatively small salary and large commission.

This doesn't mean that the help of a tied agent may never be useful to you. For example, if you know from independent research and comparison shopping that you want to buy an insurance policy offered by a particular company, a tied agent for that company can answer specific questions about the policy, help you make the purchase, submit the proper forms and so on. However, the burden is on you to arrive at an independent decision as to which financial products you want to consider, and preferably to do so *before* consulting with a tied agent. However, if you know exactly what you want, you could go directly to a discount broker if it offers the product.

Solicitors and accountants. Some lawyers and accountants offer financial planning as part of their professional services work. Their professional training makes them particularly well equipped to focus on specific aspects of the financial world. For instance, there are solicitors who specialise in tax-saving strategies, estate-planning techniques, small-business finance and other legal matters related to your money. The more specific you can be in describing the kind of legal or accounting guidance you need, the easier it will be for you to find just the right professional to help you. Don't assume that any solicitor or accountant is qualified to advise you on financial matters: seek out a specialist who has devoted himself to mastering the field in which you need help.

Stockbrokers. At some point in your financial life, you will probably need to work with a stockbroker. A broker acts as a middleman between an individual and the investment market. He handles the purchase and sale of securities, keeps track of the flow of dividends and other investment income into your account, maintains financial records for you and otherwise helps you navigate – and hopefully profit from – the investment markets. Some brokers work independently; others work for financial firms that employ many brokers, maintain multiple offices and provide information and services via phone and Internet as well as in person.

There are three main kinds of brokers:

Execution-only brokers simply buy and sell shares or other securities on your behalf, for which they are paid a small commission. They offer no financial or investment advice. The cheapest execution-only brokers now make it easy for investors to manage their investments on the Internet, entering buy or sell decisions with just a few clicks on the keyboard at any hour of the day or night. They're called *online brokers,* and they offer an excellent, convenient service for investors who understand how markets work, know their financial goals and risk tolerance and have a good idea as to the kinds of investments they want to buy.

Advisory brokers handle your trades, just as execution-only brokers do. However, they also offer investment ideas and advice. Since your broker usually handles most or all of your investment transactions and maintains your financial records, he knows your portfolio well and is in a good position to suggest ways of helping it grow. After he works with you a while, he should develop a good sense of your money personality – your risk tolerance, your interests and objectives and the kinds of investments you have confidence in.

Many advisory brokers also have access to a wealth of useful investment information. Through the brokerage houses that employ them, they can get their hands on company reports, analysts' assessments of a firm's financial prospects and its quality of management, and strategic memos prepared by experts on all manner of financial topics – interest rates, foreign developments, new business sectors, economic cycles and so on. Thus, an advisory broker can help accelerate your financial education.

It's a little more expensive to work with an advisory broker than with an execution-only broker, since the commissions you pay on trades must also cover the costs of maintaining the brokerage company's research department. However, for most investors just starting out, and for those who don't have the time, energy or desire to become experts on investing, an advisory broker is a good choice.

If you employ an advisory broker, take full advantage of the research and advice he can offer. When you're curious about a particular business sector or a company that's issuing shares or other securities, ask your broker for information. He will probably have some research to send you: an analyst's report, a printout of company financial data, or the like. He may also suggest other similar investments that are worth examining for comparison's sake. And he may have advice to offer based on the experience of other clients with these investments.

It's great when your broker provides research ideas and information. But always remember that *you* must make the final investment decisions. Sometimes investors feel intimidated by their brokers or obligated to follow their advice because of the time and effort they've expended in generating investment ideas. Don't! Remember: providing you with investment information is part of your broker's job, for which he gets well paid. You mustn't worry about hurting his feelings if you decide not to invest at all or to invest in something different.

Some experienced investors find it useful to maintain two brokerage accounts – one with an execution-only broker, one with an advisory broker. They keep a part of their investment portfolio in each account. The advisory broker serves as a source of information and ideas, while the execution-only broker is used as an inexpensive way of carrying out buy or sell orders on which no special advice is needed. This is an option you may want to consider as your self-confidence and experience grow.

The third type of broker, the *portfolio manager*, is generally employed only by the wealthy. In addition to executing trades requested by his clients, he actually makes investment decisions on their behalf and has discretionary authority over the account. The portfolio manager and the client may agree together on a general set of goals and investment strategies, but all the details are left up to the manager, who simply reports his results to the client periodically. Hence the alternative name for the portfolio broker, the *discretionary broker,* since he has the written discretionary authority to act on your behalf. He is generally paid a significant fee, sometimes based on a percentage of the total amount of money invested.

Naturally, it's not possible for a broker to act in this capacity unless the client has given him legal authorisation to spend and invest money on their behalf. While there are many good discretionary brokers, this kind of arrangement is *not* recommended for the average investor. You must know the broker very well and have nothing less than absolute, implicit trust in him.

If your beloved Uncle Nigel has been successfully managing the family fortune for the past 40 years, then *maybe* you should give him the power of trading on your behalf. If anyone less trustworthy asks for that power, don't be afraid to say no!

Finding and Choosing a Financial Adviser

Where should you start looking for an adviser? If a friend or family member raves about their IFA or broker, that's a good starting point. Personal recommendations are often the best bet. Remember, however, that no two people have exactly the same financial needs, experience level or investment styles. The adviser who suits your cousin or your next-door neighbour to a T may simply 'feel wrong' to you. In that case, follow your instincts and keep searching rather than settling for someone you aren't comfortable with.

If you don't have any personal connections to build on, you can find an IFA in your area by using the website www.unbiased.co.uk. This service will give a number of recommendations based on your postcode and the type of advice you're looking for.

Once you have the names of a couple of advisers, there are a number of specific credentials to look for. Look for an adviser with the letters AFPC or DipPFS after his name. This means he has earned the advanced financial planning certificate, which requires a significant amount of experience and background knowledge. A Certified Financial Planner (CFP) credential is now the gold standard. For retirement planning advice, ask any adviser you are considering whether or not he has passed pensions exam G60, or the JO4 and JO5 which have replaced it. An independent financial adviser has to be registered by the FSA before they can give financial advice, while a financial firm has to be authorised by the FSA. Other credentials some advisers have include memberships in APCIMS (the Association of Private Client Investment Managers), ASIM (the Association of Solicitors) and Investment Managers), AIFA (the Association of Independent Financial Advisers) and the CII (Chartered Insurance Institute). If they are members of the Institute of Financial Planning (IFP) it means they are Certified Financial Planners. These are advisers who take a holistic approach to financial planning and are licensed by the IFP. You can find out which firms are authorised by the FSA by checking the consumer section of their website (www.fsa.gov.uk). The same website also contains information about complaints against specific advisers, which is worth checking before settling on a particular choice.

Credentials are only one element in choosing an adviser. The personal fit between you and an adviser is equally important. Here are some tips about how to get a feeling for this fit.

Start by having a chat on the phone with a potential adviser. If you find him congenial, helpful and courteous, ask for a preliminary face-to-face meeting. Many advisers will offer the first meeting as a free service, but ask about this in your phone call. Then, before you go to the meeting, review your current financial situation:

- As I explained in previous chapters, find out what kind of State Pension you will be eligible for and how much you can expect to receive.

133

- Determine the status of your occupational pensions and personal pensions, if any.
- Decide the age at which you want to retire, and be prepared to explain, at least in general terms, the kind of lifestyle you hope to enjoy after retirement.
- Prepare a list of all financial products you own, including savings accounts, shares, ISAs, insurance policies and unit trusts. If you own a business, a home or other properties, list those, including your best estimate of their current value. It will be helpful if you take along documentation relating to endowments, life insurance policies and any other pensions.
- Consider how you feel about risk – specifically, the degree of risk you'd be willing to accept in exchange for potentially higher investment returns.

Thinking about these things before your first meeting, and bringing with you a folder of basic information on all these matters, will help make your conversation with the adviser informative and useful.

Here are some of the most important topics to discuss during your first meeting with a potential adviser:

- **Fees and commissions.** If you want to pay a fee, ask the hourly rate and request an estimate of how many hours it would take to arrange a pension fund for you. (The adviser may defer this question until the end of the meeting, at which time he will have a better sense as to how complex your situation is.) If you would prefer to pay by commission, ask how this is determined. In some cases, the commission is a one-time fee, for example, the cost of setting up a personal pension might be 6 or 7 per cent of the first year's contributions. In other cases, there are ongoing charges, such as an initial commission of 3 per cent and 'renewal commission' of perhaps 0.5 per cent for every year you keep contributing to your retirement fund.

- **Professional experience.** Ask the adviser how long he has been working in the field. At least ten years' experience is desirable, since this means he has advised clients in both positive and negative market conditions. Also ask about his experiences with other clients in a similar position to you, and request a couple of personal referrals – satisfied customers you can speak with who will describe their experiences with the adviser.

- **Working style.** Ask the adviser to describe his preferred manner of interacting with clients. Can you call on the phone or email with questions and concerns? (Some advisers are more willingly available than others; the response to this question should tell you which category this adviser falls into.) How frequently will the adviser review your holdings and meet you to discuss adjustments? (A dedicated adviser will recommend such a review at least once a year.) Will the adviser call you with investment ideas, or will he wait for you to contact him with suggestions or questions? (Either approach may be acceptable, so long as you understand the programme and are prepared to take on the appropriate level of responsibility.) When your adviser is on holiday or otherwise unavailable, who will take your calls and provide you with service? (Some advisers work with partners, who may end up playing significant roles in handling your account. You may want to meet the partners before making a final choice of adviser.)

- **Preliminary advice.** You may want to ask an adviser you are considering, 'Suppose I were to give you one quarter of my savings' (or some other appropriate amount) 'and ask you to invest it for me. What sorts of investments do you think you would recommend?' The answer will be revealing – not so much for the specific securities mentioned by the adviser, but as for the manner in which he formulates and communicates a response. Does he base his answer on a reasonably detailed evaluation of your personal circumstances and goals, or do you sense that he is offering you a 'one-size-fits-all' recommendation? Does he explain the reasoning behind his choices in clear, understandable language, or does he couch it in jargon that discourages questions?

Pay attention to the way you *feel* as the conversation progresses. You must choose an adviser with whom you feel comfortable. Money is an emotional topic. You want an adviser with whom you can be honest about your fears, dreams and desires; whom you can question repeatedly, if necessary, to understand your options; whom you can disagree with and, when appropriate, overrule; and whom you can challenge or criticise, when necessary, without feeling intimidated or embarrassed.

In this preliminary conversation, the potential adviser should also be evaluating and learning about you. He should ask about your family and work circumstances, your long-range goals, the age at which you want to retire, the level of retirement income you want and your risk tolerance, including how much you could afford to lose in a worst-case scenario. He should also ask about your current financial situation, your investment experience, your existing pension plans and your savings programme. An adviser who doesn't bother to inquire about these details, or who appears uninterested in them, may be more interested in selling you some high-commission, off-the-shelf product than in tailoring a financial plan to your needs.

As you can see, choosing a financial adviser is no simple matter; it takes homework, planning, thought and time. But you'll find this a worthwhile investment of energy. Having an adviser you really trust and whom you can work with for years to come provides an enormous amount of peace of mind and can make a big difference in the success of your retirement programme.

Working with Your Adviser

Having chosen a financial adviser, expect to invest some time and effort in making the relationship productive. Don't assume that your retirement programme can go on autopilot, with little or no attention from you. Changing personal circumstances, shifting economic conditions, and fluctuations in investment performance all demand regular reviews of your financial plan, and you owe it to yourself to play an active role in this process. Most of the (thankfully rare) horror stories one hears about abused or defrauded investors begin with an attitude of passivity: 'I had no idea what my broker was doing . . . I never asked any questions . . . I didn't understand, but I assumed . . .'

Don't fall into the passivity trap. Your chance of maintaining a successful and happy relationship with your adviser will be much greater if you:

- **Keep complete, accurate records of your transactions.** Start a file in which you store all your financial paperwork and keep it up to date.
- **Track your financial results.** Review the decisions you've made periodically to evaluate their success or failure, as shown by the growth of your money – or its failure to grow. This is crucial if you hope to learn from your wins and losses and gradually sharpen your financial skills.
- **Make notes of your conversations with your adviser.** Be sure you capture your adviser's suggestions, advice and warnings accurately. Otherwise, you are bound to make mistakes. Worse still, you'll never be certain whether your

investment gains (or losses) are occurring because of your adviser's help or *in spite of* it.

- **Keep your adviser fully informed.** Tell your adviser about changes in your financial status, goals, needs and wishes. Let him know how you're feeling about your money and the markets. And speak up when your objectives, your risk tolerance or your interests change.
- **Stay abreast of the news.** Keep yourself generally informed about financial and economic trends. Read the business pages of your newspaper and discuss with your adviser how the latest developments may affect your personal investments and financial plans.
- **Ask questions!** Make sure you understand the risks and costs before you agree to any investment or other financial plan. If your adviser insists on using technical jargon and can't or won't translate it into plain, understandable English, consider changing advisers.

For his part, your adviser should always:

- **Practise full disclosure.** Your adviser should explain both the risks and the potential benefits from any financial strategy he is proposing. Remember, no investment is completely risk-free. Run away from any adviser who claims to offer one that is.
- **Explain all costs.** Your adviser must be able and willing to explain the commissions, fees and other expenses associated with a proposed investment. Insist on a clear answer, not a vague one.
- **Understand your circumstances.** Your adviser should be able to explain how and why a proposed investment or other strategy is suitable for *your* financial goals, risk tolerance and other personal characteristics. A cookie-cutter approach is *never* the best.

- **Describe your right to change your mind.** Many financial products – though not all! – are required to provide a cooling-off period during which a new investor may cancel and receive a full refund.
- **Provide regular written reports.** You should receive notices showing the current performance of your investments as well as any transactions from the most recent time period. If you have difficulty understanding every detail on these reports, your adviser should be willing and able to explain them to you in plain English.

However, for a happy financial relationship, you *shouldn't* expect a financial adviser to:

- **Make investment decisions for you**, unless you specifically authorise and ask him to do so. And as I've suggested, this is generally *not* a good idea. It's your money! Stay in control.
- **Assume investment risk on your behalf.** If the adviser informs you honestly and accurately about the risks involved in any investment decision, then losses you may suffer as a result of those risks are simply part of the price of being an investor – not something you can blame on the adviser or expect him to repay.
- **Stop you from making decisions that are ill-advised or inappropriate.** If you insist on choosing a particular investment or strategy despite receiving reasonable notice about its disadvantages from your adviser, then you alone are to blame for the consequences.
- **Remember every detail of your life and situation.** Be realistic in your expectations about your adviser's memory and mastery of your circumstances. Be prepared, if necessary, to remind your adviser of any relevant data about yourself: 'Are you sure I ought to be moving a lot of

money out of cash right now? Remember my daughter is starting university next autumn and there will be big tuition bills to pay.'

- **Hold your hand or play psychiatrist.** Managing money can be emotionally trying. If you find yourself becoming unduly anxious, fearful, confused or angry when the value of investments changes, don't take out your moods on your financial adviser. Don't demand hourly phone calls or long meetings to commiserate about your financial woes. Instead, if you find yourself unable to sleep at night because your investments are too volatile, consider moving your money into less-risky vehicles (when the timing is right).

When a Dispute Arises

The suggestions I've given above should help you create and maintain a positive, rewarding relationship with your financial adviser. But as in any human relationship, misunderstandings and conflicts will sometimes arise. When this happens, take a deep breath. There are a number of specific steps you can take to minimise the problems and maximise your chances of resolving the issues in a way that will take only a small toll on your sanity and your bank account.

If you feel that your financial adviser has been giving you poor advice, neglecting you, misleading you or even lying to you, start by describing your complaint directly to him in writing. (Too many people register their complaints by phone call with no written follow-up. They rarely have the dispute resolved to their liking.) In your letter, explain exactly what is troubling you and suggest an appropriate remedy – for example, a refund of an excessive fee or commission that you've been charged, or a cost-free transfer of your funds from the investment you didn't want into the one you intended to choose. If the problem arose from a simple misunderstanding or a minor error, this should suffice to correct it.

If not, you can move up the chain of command within the company that employs your adviser (unless, of course, he runs a one-person shop). Most financial service companies have well-established procedures for handling client complaints, and if your unhappiness is well-grounded, the firm may be willing to waive fees or reimburse small losses in order to keep you as a customer.

If you're still not satisfied with how your complaint is resolved, take it to the relevant independent complaint organisation. The Financial Ombudsman Service deals with complaints about most financial matters (get in touch at www.financial-ombudsman.org.uk or by phoning 0300 123 9 123). Alternatively, you may want to request FSA's booklet *Guide to Making a Complaint*, online at moneymadeclear.fsa.gov.uk or by phoning 0300 500 5000.

Taking Charge of Your Own Financial Future

Above all, remember that your financial future, including your retirement programme, is *your* responsibility. It's your money and your life, and no one else – not your broker, IFA, accountant or solicitor – will ever care about it as much as you do,

I know you're busy. Work, school, family activities, social obligations – all of these demand ever-increasing pieces of your mind and your time. It would be lovely to delegate portions of your life to others and never have to worry about them again.

Unfortunately, this usually doesn't work, as millions of people have come to realise. That is why self-reliance is increasingly in vogue. More and more working people are charting their own careers through self-employment and freelancing rather than relying on the support of a paternalistic corporation. More and more parents are taking charge of their children's education rather than assuming that 'teacher knows best'. And more and more medical patients are researching their ailments online and exploring unconventional remedies like herbal cures and acupuncture rather than passively accepting a doctor's prescriptions and hoping for the best.

The self-help approach to life is certainly more demanding than depending on the wisdom of hired experts. But it may also produce better results. You need to apply the same philosophy to planning your financial future.

However, if you are not the sole captain steering the ship of your financial future (and most of us are not), I suggest you stay very close to the broker or financial adviser who is helping to captain your ship. Remember: your relationship with this person is a partnership.

7. Turns in the Road:
Monitoring and Adjusting Your Plan

Keeping Tabs

You've got a nice pension fund up and running, with payments going into it every month and your investments growing regularly. Congratulations! You're ahead of many others and well on your way to enjoying a successful retirement. Take a moment to pat yourself on the back. But don't go to sleep entirely. If you do, you may wake up at the age of 65 to find that your carefully laid plans have gone awry. Circumstances change, economic conditions shift, the stock market fluctuates and government pension rules are revised. It's important to make sure that your retirement plans keep up with the times, rather than become out of date.

One element in keeping tabs on your retirement plans is simply making sure that you get regular updates on the growth of your money. You should be getting statements from the company that manages your pension investment at least once a year. And each statement should be a reminder to you to recheck your calculations to make sure that your funds are on track to create the nest egg you need.

Pension statements used to be fairly baffling, full of jargon and unfathomable calculations. Many people stuck them straight in a filing cabinet or in the back of a desk drawer. However, legislation in 2003 ordered pension providers to make their statements easier to understand, providing all the information you need to see how your plan is growing in simple terms. (Unfortunately, these regulations apply only to money-purchase schemes. However, if you have a final salary scheme, you should receive statements that show your expected pension as a percentage of your current salary. Remember that the amount shown is in today's money, but it should rise in line with inflation every year, and it will change depending on what your 'final salary' is.)

Here's an illustration of how one of today's modern, easy-to-read money-purchase pension statements might look.

Your Pension Fund Statement

Your name: Jack Sprat

Your date of birth: 6 April 1960

Your plan number: C13579468

Your National Insurance number: KL 00 00 00 X

The date you joined the scheme was: 1 July 1990

The effective date of this statement is: 1 July 2008

Contributions paid into your pension this year:

You have paid into your pension: £2,847

Your employer has paid into your pension: £1,500

The government has paid in tax relief: £803

The value of your pension fund so far:

The value of your fund at 1 July 2008 is: £105,489

Your future pension:

To illustrate your possible future pension we have assumed that:

- Your retirement date is: 6 April 2025

- You will continue to pay contributions until your retirement date at the rate of 10% of earnings including tax relief from the government. The earnings on which contributions are based were £36,500 at 1 July 2008.

The estimated pension when you retire is: £25,507 a year

If you have any questions, you can phone us on: 0845 555-5555
Or email us on: questions@xyzpension.com.uk

When you receive your pension statement, scan it to make sure it is accurate. Look at the figures for this year's contributions, and make sure they match the amounts that have been deducted from your pay cheque for the plan. Compare the statement to the previous one, and make sure that your money is growing incrementally as it should.

Then follow the steps below to make sure that your overall retirement planning is still on track to meet your long-term goals.

1. Request an updated forecast from the Department for Work and Pensions to confirm the estimated value of your State Pension and S2P entitlements.

2. Add up the totals of all your retirement investments, including savings accounts, share and bond holdings, unit trusts and ISAs.

3. Check the total against the nest egg target you calculated in chapter 4. Are you making progress towards achieving that goal? If your investments continue to grow at the current pace between now and your expected retirement date, will you amass the savings you need to fund your retirement?

I suggest you create a chart like the one shown on page 147. Use it to track the annual growth of your retirement nest egg, reflecting both the contributions to savings that you make each year and the increase in value of your investments. Using a calculator, you can also figure out how your nest egg is likely to grow in the future. Factor in the amount of savings you are setting aside each year, as well as an estimated rate of investment growth. Base your estimate growth rate on the current performance of your investments. If most of your investments are in shares, you might want to assume an annual growth rate of 7 per cent. (This is actually less than the long-term growth rate of share investments in the UK, which, as I mentioned earlier, has averaged about 12 per cent per year over the past four decades.) If you prefer to be even more conservative, use 5 per cent. If your investments grow a bit faster than you anticipate, you will be ahead of the game. In a few minutes, you should be able to determine whether or not your retirement savings plan is on track or falling short.

In the sample table shown, the retirement nest egg being tracked has grown from £7,380 in its first year (20 years before retirement) to over £118,000 in its current year (ten years before retirement). This growth has occurred thanks to two things: an annual increase in investment value averaging 7 per cent, and contributions from earnings of £7,500 per year. To estimate next year's value, you would multiply the current value by 1.07 (which is the equivalent of 7 per cent growth), then add £7,500.

If you perform this calculation ten times, you'll find that the current £118,141 will grow to £336,026. That's how big this nest egg will be ten years from now, on the expected retirement date.

Will this nest egg grow at *exactly* this rate? Almost surely not. Some years, the investments will do better – they may grow in value by 10 or 14 per cent rather than 7 per cent. Other years, they will do worse – they may grow by only 4 per cent, or even lose value. But over time, if the portfolio is invested in a well-chosen collection of shares or unit trusts with a reasonable degree of risk, the growth of the nest egg should be close to an annual average of 7 per cent, or perhaps a bit more.

Retirement Nest Egg Growth (Sample)

Years to retirement	Current nest egg value
20	£7,380
19	£15,397
18	£23,975
17	£33,153
16	£42,974
15	£53,482
14	£64,726
13	£76,756
12	£89,629
11	£103,403
10	£118,141

If you perform these calculations and discover that your nest egg is on track to reach the target size you estimated earlier, all is well. However, if your nest egg appears likely to fall short of the amount you need, you'll have to make some adjustments.

There are two basic options to consider if you need to increase the growth of your nest egg. One is to look for ways to improve your investment growth. Look closely at your portfolio and determine whether your investment choices are the right ones for you. Is most or all of your money invested in relatively slow-growth, low-risk securities, such as gilts, bond trusts, corporate bonds and blue-chip shares? If so, consider moving a portion of your portfolio into securities with slightly greater risk and slightly higher growth potential, such as mid-cap shares or unit trusts that invest in such shares. But be careful. Do your homework before investing in risky securities, work closely with a trusted financial adviser, and don't put so much of your portfolio at risk that you find it hard to sleep at night!

The other option is to increase the amount you save every year. This is always a safer option, and the closer you are to retirement, the more attractive it is. (As I've discussed, if you are just a few years away from retirement, you don't want to have most of your money in risky investment vehicles; you don't want to take the chance of retiring at a time when the market is in a down cycle, thereby depressing the value of your portfolio.) If you've been saving £2,500 per year for retirement, up it to £3,500; if you've been saving £5,000, stretch to make it £7,000. The bigger the chunk of money you can squirrel away every year, the better your chances of reaching your personal magic number.

More Rules of Retirement-Plan Maintenance

In addition to monitoring the growth of your pension investments and making adjustments as needed, there are some other basic steps you need to follow to make sure your retirement plans remain current and effective.

Periodically reconsider your S2P participation. As I explained in chapter 3, the State Second Pension (S2P) is a government programme that you may or may not choose to participate in. Your choice should depend on whether or not you can enjoy better investment performance through an occupational or personal pension. Once a year, get a new State Pension forecast and reconsider whether you should opt in or out of S2P. In addition, you may want to revisit your decision any time the government announces changes to S2P regulations as well. Ask your financial adviser if necessary. [Note: S2P will stop in 2012 and be replaced by a single flat rate.]

Review your investment choices at least once per year. Most investments, especially in shares, have a natural life span. As conditions change, a company that was formerly an attractive purchase eventually becomes less attractive. Review your investment portfolio annually and decide whether some of the securities you own should be sold in favour of new holdings. Do you own shares of a once-hot company that has grown quickly for five years but is now slowing down? Does growth in a single business sector mean that you now own huge amounts of shares in one industry? Have your investments in shares, bonds and other securities become out of balance? All of these can be good reasons to sell some investments and buy others.

Reconsider your lifestyle assumptions. At the same time you review your investment performance, go back and think about the retirement plans you drew up at the start of the process. Do they still make sense, or has your definition of 'the good life' changed? Have there been dramatic swings in prices (for example, for real estate) that could force you to revise your plans as to where and how you will live? Have changes in your health or your work status caused you to reconsider your thinking about when – or whether – you will stop working? You may want to modify the tentative budget you drew up for your post-retirement years, which in turn may require adjustments in the size of the nest egg you need to build.

These universal issues require everyone to re-examine their retirement plans at least once a year. But others may need to make changes at different times, sometimes at unpredictable intervals. In the next few pages, I'll focus on some special circumstances that demand careful reconsideration of retirement options. One or more of these may apply to you.

When You Get Married

If you get married or move in with someone, you'll probably want to alter your pension to include your new partner. Failure to do this can cause serious complications later on, when (as will likely happen) one of you dies first.

Many women now in their 60s left financial planning to their husbands. This was a cultural norm, further encouraged by the fact that most men in that generation enjoyed greater earning power than most women. However, since men have a shorter life expectancy than women, there are more widows than widowers around, and many of those widows are now finding themselves facing a steep learning curve as they try to master the intricacies of retirement planning, pensions and annuities. A widow can be in for an unpleasant shock if it turns out that her husband wasn't quite such a wizard with numbers as she had thought.

This happened to Mabel. After her husband Harry died at the age of 65, she discovered that he'd built up a 'single-life' pension, and she wasn't entitled to a penny of it. Harry meant no harm; a single-life pension is cheaper than a joint-life one, and it's quite likely that Harry simply overlooked the fine print or misunderstood what a financial salesperson told him. But whatever the reason, Mabel's retirement plans took quite a blow. At 63, she had to go back to work in a chemist's shop just to keep a roof over her head.

Another couple, Helen and David, now in their 80s, are desperately worried that Helen will die first. As it happens, she was the bigger earner in their working days, and she has a decent-sized but non-transferable pension. David, by contrast, has only a minuscule retirement fund and would struggle to live on it by himself. What a shame that this worry is blighting their last years together.

The lesson of both cases is clear: if you want a partner or spouse to receive your pension after you die, make sure the policy documents specify it. In most cases, it won't happen automatically.

Most pension providers will pay out at least the value of your fund to your spouse if you die before retirement age. Many occupational pension schemes include life insurance coverage while you are working and a pension for your spouse and any dependent children after your death. However, the payments specified may be only a percentage of the pension you'll receive while you're alive; check the individual policy.

With personal pension schemes and stakeholder pensions, you can choose to contribute extra in order to provide for a partner (by buying a joint-life annuity) if you die after retirement. Check with your financial adviser or the company that manages your pension to find out how much more such coverage will cost, or shop around for a company offering the best rates for a joint-life annuity. If your partner is much younger than you, the cost could be substantial. In that case, you might want to consider another alternative: choosing a single-life pension supplemented by a substantial life insurance policy to help support your partner after your death.

State Pension entitlements can be transferable between husband and wife and civil partners. A widow or widower who doesn't qualify for a State Pension in their own right can inherit their spouse's entitlement. They can also inherit up to 50 per cent of SERPS or S2P contributions. However, you can't have both your partner's pension and your own; instead, you should choose the bigger pot and apply for it.

If You Get Divorced

If you get divorced, you'll need to make sure any pension owned by either partner is split fairly in the settlement. There are various ways this can be done:

- The value of the pension can be offset against another portion of the couple's total assets. For example, if one partner hangs onto the pension, the other gets to take something else of equivalent value, like the house. The financial split is equitable, but the partner without a pension will have to scramble to create one before retirement, while the partner without a house will have to find somewhere to live.
- Alternatively, the partner without a pension may be given a reasonable lump sum with which to start one, provided there is sufficient cash available or if cash can be raised from the sale of a house.
- As another option, the court can earmark part of an existing pension for the benefit of the ex-spouse. For example, part of the retirement lump sum as well as a fraction of the monthly income the pension provides can be set aside for the former wife or husband. This choice is not popular with divorcing couples; among other disadvantages, it prolongs the time the couple have to continue dealing with each other.
- Finally, the pension can be split between the two parties, with part of the cash value transferred to create a new scheme for the ex-spouse. There are administrative costs associated with this option, but at least it allows each partner to walk away with his or her pension.

In most cases, both partners are financially worse off after a divorce, and this fact of life applies to pensions as well. After the split, you will probably have to plan on increasing your pension contributions to get your savings rate back up to the level you need in order to enjoy a reasonable retirement.

When You Change Jobs

Nowadays, few people stay with the same employer throughout an entire working life. What should you do about your occupational pension scheme when you change your job? Provided you have belonged to the scheme for two years or more, you have several options:

- You can leave the pension you have built up in your old employer's fund and collect it when you retire. This is known as a 'preserved' or frozen pension. If it's a money-purchase scheme, the fund will continue to grow, although no new contributions will be paid in. If it's a final salary scheme, your pension will be worked out using the formula that takes into account the number of years you were with the company and your salary when you left. The administrators of the company plan will be able to tell you about how your pension works and the amount of money you can expect to receive when you retire.
- Alternatively, you might be able to transfer your old employer's pension to your new employer's scheme. This will be simpler if you are transferring from one money-purchase scheme to another. If you transfer a final salary scheme, the terms may not be beneficial, and it would be worthwhile to seek professional advice.
- If your new employer doesn't have an occupational scheme, leave your previous pension with your old employer and start a new personal or stakeholder plan

(either via your employer or on your own) to build up
future retirement savings.

- If you are leaving an employer who does not offer an
  occupational pension scheme and moving to one who
  does, you'll need to consider your options carefully. If you
  have an existing stakeholder or personal pension scheme,
  investigate whether joining the occupational scheme will
  be beneficial. Where your employer makes contributions
  on your behalf, it generally will be. Can you afford to do
  both? Most personal pensions follow stakeholder rules
  and don't penalise you for stopping or restarting
  contributions, but check with yours.

If you've been with your employer for less than two years
when you leave, you may be forced to cash in your contributions. Alternatively, you might be able to preserve your pension
in the old employer's fund or to transfer it to the new employer.

People who change jobs several times in their working life
often leave behind a paper trail of small pension funds. It's
important to keep track of them – after all, each one represents
a packet of money you've contributed to and which you are
entitled to receive when you retire.

In theory, you should be contacted by the pension management firm when you reach retirement age. In practice, however,
old pensions have a way of getting lost. People move, they change
their names and companies are sold, merge or go bankrupt. As
a result, tracking down the pension from that job you left 15 years
ago may be tricky. For help, contact the Pensions Tracing Service,
a government agency charged with providing this assistance to
UK citizens. You can reach them either at their website
(http://www.thepensionservice.gov.uk/atoz/atozdetailed/pension
tracing.asp) or by telephone (0845 600 2537).

Finally, if you have a period of unemployment for whatever

reason, try to keep up your payments to a personal pension plan (more on this important topic below).

When You Have Missing Years

Many people have gaps in their pension contributions record. It can happen for any number of reasons. Perhaps you stayed at home for two or three years to bring up young children or to look after an elderly or disabled relative; maybe you were made redundant and spent a period unemployed; you may have had an accident that prevented you from working; or it might be that you fell into debt and stopped making pension contributions while working off your credit card bills. Whatever the reason, once you get back on track, you'll have some catching up to do if you hope to be able to retire on time – or even behind time.

My first recommendation: avoid gaps in pension contributions if at all possible. However, if you experience difficulties that make it impossible to keep up your contributions – such as unemployment or a disabling illness – talk to your stakeholder or personal pension provider. (Stakeholder pensions have to let you stop and start payments whenever you like.)

Once you are ready to resume pension contributions after a period of neglect, you will want to boost your savings by a notch or two. Make sacrifices to increase your contributions or stash lump sum payments in your fund if at all possible. Remember the importance of compound interest and the magical power of having time on your side. The sooner you deposit a pound into your investment account, the sooner it can begin to grow on your behalf – and the larger it will become by the time you need to depend on it.

An employment record with years off may also affect your State Pension coverage. When you request your pension forecast from the Department for Work and Pensions, you'll learn whether or not you are entitled to a full pension. If you are short of the number of the years needed to qualify you for a full pension, you may be able to pay voluntary contributions to make up some or all of the difference. (An adviser at the Pension Service can walk you through this option.)

What's more, if you have missing years because you've been a carer of some sort, you might be eligible to 'skip' years under a scheme called Home Responsibilities Protection (HRP). You are entitled to HRP if you are caring for a child, been a foster carer or been looking after a seriously ill or disabled person. Each year during which you have these 'home responsibilities' will be deducted from the number of qualifying years you need to get a full State Pension. However, you will still need at least 20 years' contributions to receive the full amount. The government plans to replace HRP with a more flexible 'carer's credit' in 2010.

It's essential that women who plan to have children in future should think ahead when making their pension arrangements. If you think you will have a broken employment record, a stakeholder pension will probably be your best option. You would also be well advised *not* to contract out of S2P. Alternatively, choose a final salary scheme that will pay you a guaranteed amount in retirement and top up your National Insurance contributions to get the full state entitlement. In most cases, a scheme that gives you a set amount per month after you retire will be better than a money-purchase scheme.

Stay in Command

The most important lesson of this chapter is a simple one. You need to stay in command of your retirement savings and investment programme. Don't assume you can open an account or two, sign on with a financial adviser and then leave your money on autopilot. There are too many ways for the best-laid plans to go astray, and only you have the knowledge and interest necessary to keep them focused on your needs and goals.

Fortunately, the amount of time and energy required is modest. Create a file for records and documents related to your retirement plan. Use it to store all your transaction receipts, account statements and pension forecasts, as well as the worksheets and charts you've created while working through this book. At least once a year, pull out this file and review the current status of your retirement programme.

This works best if you establish a routine for your 'annual financial check-up'. Many people like to do it during January, the start of a new year. Others prefer springtime ('spring cleaning'), the autumn (when the school year traditionally begins) or around their own birthdays. Whatever time of year you choose, arrange a reminder: jot down the date whenever you start a new personal calendar or appointment book, or enter it in your computer.

Then, at the appointed time, work your way through the steps outlined in this chapter. Make any adjustments needed to keep your retirement savings and investment programme on track – or to get it back on track if you've veered off course. It's a simple process that will give you an amazing amount of peace of mind.

8. The Home Stretch:
What to Do as Retirement Nears

Stay Vigilant

Throughout this book, I've emphasised the importance of taking charge of your personal financial future rather than passively assuming that the government or your employer will do it for you. This advice is doubly important during the last five years of your working life, as retirement draws near.

If you're at this stage, now is no time to take your eye off the ball. Regular check-ups into your retirement plan should be part of your life routine. Increase the frequency of your reviews from annually to quarterly, and don't hesitate to take steps as needed to ensure the safety of your funds and to make up for any savings shortfalls that appear to be looming.

The decisions you make in the final months before you retire can have quite a dramatic effect on your income for the rest of your life. They could mean the difference between having to watch the pennies in your twilight years or being able to afford a few more treats. I know which I would prefer.

The sooner you anticipate a savings shortfall, the more time you'll have to rectify it and the less painful it will be to make it up. In most cases – particularly during the last five years prior to retirement – the key to getting back on track will be increasing the amount you save and contribute to your personal or occupational pension plan.

The options you have for boosting your final years of saving will depend, in part, on the kind of pension you have. If you are a member of an occupational pension scheme, you can enjoy tax benefits while contributing as much of your salary as you can afford and the scheme will let you. If you are currently paying less than this, you can make additional voluntary contributions (AVCs) up to the total allowed, and you will enjoy immediate tax relief on each AVC. There are different ways they can work.

In a final salary scheme, you can buy extra years of membership to top up your pension. This is a good idea if you expect to stay with the same employer until your retirement, although it can be expensive. Alternatively, AVCs can be used to provide extra income in retirement. If your pension scheme has very limited investment choices for its AVCs, you may prefer to top up your pension through a personal pension instead. If your employer doesn't offer AVCs, a stakeholder pension may be a better idea.

If you have your own stakeholder or personal pension, you can top up your contributions to the limits described in chapter 3 at any time. Or you can start a separate pension scheme with another provider.

However, you don't have to use pension contributions to make up any lump sum shortfall. You could use ISAs, if the annual limits on ISA investment will let you reach your target. Or you can opt for any other kind of investment in cash, shares, bonds or property, but remember to take into account that you will have to pay tax on the profits these investments make, since they will lack the tax benefits enjoyed by pensions and ISAs.

The main thing is, do something! When you receive a retirement plan statement that contains worrisome news, don't file it in the wastebasket and put it out of your head. It's so tempting to avoid or ignore bad news. But when the economy shifts and markets change course, millions of people are affected, and each of us must respond in order to protect ourselves.

I'm speaking here from personal experience. The stock market decline that began in 2008 and continues today means that many people, including me, find their retirement plans have slipped off course. As soon as I noticed this, I took steps to remedy the shortfall. I took on extra work, although this wasn't easy (I like evenings and weekends off just as much as the next person). I also cut back on my spending, altering holiday plans, and reducing the amount I spent on luxuries such as clothes, art and eating out. Was it painful? Yes, more than a little bit. It was difficult for me to watch my investments decline in value *again,* just as they had done in 2000. But this time the drop was deeper, much deeper. I decided to keep the new money I would have invested in shares and bonds in a savings account until I felt the market had stabilised or nearly reached bottom. I'm still waiting. (I'm writing this in early 2009.) My early belt-tightening strategy means I have a somewhat bigger cash safety net through which to ride out this recession. I also took some profits on some of the shares in my retirement account and have left that money in cash (more accurately, a money market account). Like so many others, I'm definitely not on target for the date when I'd hoped to lighten up my workload. But I remain reasonably confident in my ability to make the right decisions when the markets recover, as they inevitably will. I can sleep at night, probably because I haven't lost hope that I'll be able to retire and keep my dignity and independence intact.

Of course, it's never possible to leave one's financial worries behind completely. There are always things that can go wrong. Who would have predicted the severity of the current recession or drop in property prices that has reduced nearly everyone's net worth? I might get sick and be unable to work for a while. One or more of the companies I work for might go belly-up, leaving me underemployed for a year or two. (This happened with the bankruptcy of Lehman Brothers and the crisis in the US financial sector.) Any of these eventualities could reduce my potential retirement income, so I am trying to save more than I think I will actually need to protect myself.

In today's unsettled economic climate, the best advice I can give you is to be conservative in your pension calculations. If you hear news reports that inflation is creeping towards 4 per cent, start doing your calculations based on 6 per cent inflation. If you estimate you'll need X amount to produce a liveable retirement income, try to save 10 per cent more than that amount.

The Retirement Countdown

Aside from being vigilant, here are some specific steps to take during the last five years before your planned retirement date:

- **Adjust your investment holdings to lower your risk.** As you learned in chapter 5, the risk profile of your investment portfolio should be shifted in the direction of lower risk as you near retirement. Securities that are higher on the risk ladder are more volatile – their prices tend to fluctuate more than those near the bottom of the ladder. With retirement approaching, this is a problem. You don't want to be stuck on retirement with a folder full of shares whose value has plummeted. So during the last ten to five years before you reach retirement age, move a portion of your investment holdings into less risky securities. If you own a lot of mid-cap or international shares, consider selling most of them and buying blue-chip companies instead. If your portfolio consists almost entirely of stocks, swap some of them for bonds or bond funds. Don't shift *entirely* into low or no-risk securities, since this could reduce your growth and income too drastically, but move the overall weighting of your portfolio towards the lower end of the risk ladder.
- **Pay down your debts.** As you approach retirement, try to pay off as much of the money you owe as possible,

including car loans, credit card bills and, especially, your home mortgage. If at all possible, try to pay off your mortgage completely before retiring. This will greatly reduce your living costs and free up a lot of cash every month for other expenses. If a portion of your mortgage remains due on retirement, you could use some of your retirement cash lump sum to pay it off; however, this will decrease your retirement savings and therefore your annual income. Weigh this option and its trade-offs carefully before making any decision.

- **Double-check your income expectations.** A year before you retire, get a final State Pension forecast. If there are any National Insurance contribution shortfalls, try to make these up through additional contributions. You can do this up to four months before your retirement date (though there are limits to how much you can repay and when). If you've lost track of any occupational pensions from past jobs, enlist the help of the Pension Tracing Service in tracking them down.

- **Claim your State Pensions.** Pension payments are not automatic. It's up to you to make sure you apply for them. Four months before your 65th birthday (or earlier if you're a woman born before 1955), you should be invited to claim your State and S2P pensions. If you don't receive your invitation, call State Pensions Claimline (0845 300 1084). Fill out the forms and send them back promptly to make sure your first payment arrives on time.

- **Claim any non-pension benefits you may be eligible for.** Your local authority may offer a travel card providing free or subsidised travel to those 60 or older. You may also be entitled to help with your council tax and housing benefit to assist with your rent. Ask your local authority about these benefits. Winter fuel payments are available to everyone over 60; call 0845 915 1515 to find out how much you're entitled to. The pension credit is a top-up for pensioners on a very low income. Speak to the Pension Service to find out whether you are eligible for assistance on 0800 991 234. Finally, if you are disabled and need special adaptations to your house in order to live there, your local council may be able to help with these costs.

- **Make investment decisions for your retirement savings.** Finally, as your retirement date arrives, you'll need to decide what to do with the money you've been accumulating over the past years. For many people, using most or all of the lump sum you've saved to purchase an annuity will prove to be the best choice. Others may opt for a different alternative. I'll explain more about your investment choices a little later in this chapter.

Getting excited about retirement yet? That's good! But before we look at the options you need to consider for investing your retirement savings, we need to detour into a slightly more difficult topic – the problems some people have experienced with occupational pensions from companies in trouble.

Bad Company?

The 1990s were a bad decade for pension holders. It emerged that thousands of people had been advised to take out a personal pension when they should have remained in their company scheme. Confidence in company schemes also took a battering after publishing tycoon Robert Maxwell stole £400 million from his companies' pension funds. The 1995 Pensions Act was passed in response to the Maxwell scandal. Under its terms, a pensions watchdog was created to supervise the running of occupational schemes. It is now known as the Pensions Regulator. The law requires that at least a third of the board of trustees running an occupational pension scheme must be member-nominated trustees, so their own retirement is on the line. Auditors and actuaries also have a much tougher legal responsibility to blow the whistle if they suspect foul play.

If you are enrolled in a company pension scheme, you might consider volunteering to serve on the board of trustees. That way, you can be involved in the investment decisions that are made, you can ask questions directly about anything you don't understand and you can complain loudly if you get suspicious about anything that doesn't seem quite kosher. Check out the Pensions Regulator's website for details of recent court cases over pension funds. It makes thought-provoking reading.

Unfortunately, the Pensions Regulator doesn't protect you or your pension if your company is taken over, merges, becomes insolvent or simply decides to 'wind up' (that is, terminate) a final salary pension scheme. This is covered by the Pensions Protection Fund. At least 125,000 scheme members lost out between 1997 and 2005. The Pensions Protection Fund only covers schemes that went bust after April 2005, but the government has also introduced a scheme (the Financial Assistance Scheme) to make sure these workers and pensioners receive some of the pension they were expecting.

If your company is taken over, chances are good the new bosses will want to phase out any existing pension schemes and merge them with their own. Ideally, they will offer you membership of their scheme, which is fine if the benefits are the same as or better than the ones you enjoyed with your old scheme. Check the terms you are being offered and consider how long you plan on staying with the new company. It's not going to be such a good deal if you change from a final salary scheme with the old one to a money-purchase scheme with the new, but you may find you don't have much say in the matter if the new employer decides to wind up the old scheme.

When a pension scheme is wound up, the assets are used to buy annuities for the members, either immediate ones if they have retired already or delayed annuities if they have yet to retire. It's likely that these annuities will pay less than the pensions they were expecting. Alternatively, members who are not already receiving their pensions may be offered a 'cash equivalent transfer value', but this is seldom enough to purchase the pensions they were expecting.

If a pension scheme is 'frozen' – another change that often occurs when a company is merged with another or simply faces financial hardships – it means that the scheme is closed to new members. A lot of companies are now deciding to freeze their final salary schemes because they have become too expensive to run. Money in a frozen scheme is still legally under the control of the scheme trustees. You'll need to track closely what happens to your pension under these circumstances, and be prepared to complain to your employer and to your government representatives if your interests are compromised.

If your company becomes insolvent (bankrupt), the insolvency practitioner will generally appoint a trustee to look after the interests of pension scheme members. The scheme will normally be wound up and, if there are sufficient resources, the trustee will either buy annuities for members of a money-purchase scheme or offer cash-equivalent transfer values for those in final salary schemes. Unfortunately, this process will usually operate at an agonising snail's pace, leaving thousands of people worrying and wondering about their future prospects. Those who have already retired will get priority over those who are still at work.

It does mean that if a pension scheme is wound up and it's found that there aren't enough assets to meet its bills, the Pension Protection Fund (supported by a levy on employers)should pay pensioners up to 90 per cent of the money they would have received up to certain limits. Certain conditions have to be met relating to the type of pension scheme and its size (e.g. schemes with only one member aren't eligible).

What should you do if you have lost out as a result of a company scheme being wound up? Complain! Complain loudly, complain clearly and keep complaining until you get the outcome you want (or as close to it as you can possibly get). If it transpires that your occupational scheme has been run fraudulently, then the Fraud Compensation Fund should reimburse all members (only up to 90 per cent for most).

To make a complaint about your occupational scheme at work, first raise it with the pensions administrator in your office. Start by mentioning it verbally, then put your complaint in writing if it's not resolved straight away. Under the 1995 Pensions Act, the company must have a standard complaints procedure and they must reply to your concerns within two months.

If you are not satisfied, you can complain to the trustees and then to The Pensions Advisory Service (TPAS), a voluntary scheme that provides advice on occupational pensions. It has an excellent website and a telephone helpline. TPAS volunteers are good at clearing up misunderstandings and can accompany you to disputes procedures, but they don't have legal powers to censure companies that are bending the rules. If there are problems TPAS can't resolve, you will be referred to the Pensions Ombudsman. The Ombudsman will hear the facts of the case and make judgments, such as ordering that you be paid compensation, which it then has the power to enforce through the courts, if necessary.

If you suspect something is illegal with the way your company pension scheme is being run, you should report them to the Pensions Regulator. Its website has useful information on what to do.

To make a complaint about a personal or stakeholder pension, you need to decide whether you think you were mis-sold the product, or if it has been badly handled since you started contributing to it. If you think you were given bad advice when you bought into the scheme and have suffered a financial loss as a result, start by contacting the firm who made the arrangements, whether it was an independent financial adviser or a representative of the company that runs the scheme.

Write to the managing director of the firm, outlining your case and explaining how you feel you have lost out as a result of their advice. Compensation should be paid if you were given wrong advice – for example, if you were advised to transfer out of an employer's occupational scheme and into a personal scheme offering less favourable returns. The compensation is likely to be paid as a contribution into your pension scheme rather than cash in hand.

You can't blame an adviser for selling you a policy that subsequently turned out to be a bad performer. No financial adviser has a crystal ball or is clairvoyant (more's the pity!). However, you may have grounds for complaint if an adviser sold you a policy that was not suitable for your circumstances – for example, if it left you exposed in high-risk areas when you had no back-up provision and the risks were not clearly explained to you. Start by reading the documentation carefully. If the warnings are there in black and white, you'll have a much weaker case. Claiming that you didn't understand what you were signing is not a valid defence in a court of law.

If you are having trouble getting satisfaction, you can take your complaint to the Financial Ombudsman Service. They will deal with complaints on your behalf and try and get them resolved, and if necessary, they have the power to force the financial company to pay compensation. To complain about your State Pension, contact the Pension Service in the first instance. If there are administrative errors they should be able to sort them out. If you don't get satisfaction from them, it can be worth seeking help from the Citizens Advice office in your area. If they think you have a good case, they might decide to do battle on your behalf, and they have more muscle than you do as an individual.

Whatever your complaint, keep copies of all correspondence relating to it and take notes of important information you received over the telephone.

Investing Your Retirement Funds: the Annuity Option

Not so long ago, practically everyone who invested in a pension scheme was required to buy an annuity on retirement or shortly thereafter. Since A-Day, more options have been created. But let's start with the annuity option, since this is still a suitable choice for most investors.

An annuity is a kind of insurance policy that provides you with income for life in return for a lump sum of cash from your pension fund. The long-term value of an annuity depends on several factors, including the interest rate in effect at the time you purchase the annuity. However, the greatest factor is your lifespan. If you live into your 90s, an annuity is likely to be a great investment for you, since the annuity provider is required to keep paying you, year after year, as long as you live. However, if you die soon after buying the annuity, the funds normally aren't passed on to your heirs but rather kept by the provider – a very bad deal for you. (It's another good reason to take care of your health: the longer you live, the more profitable your annuity investment will become!) Of course, if you purchased a joint annuity, then it will continue paying out to the surviving spouse or civil partner.

If you've been contributing to a money-purchase pension scheme, you should start researching annuity rates a year or so before your retirement date. Any insurance company will be happy to provide you with information about their annuity offerings, and there are a number of websites that provide comparative information from many providers.

Your pension provider will offer you their own annuity, but you are not bound to accept it. No matter how good it sounds, make sure you shop around and see what the competition has to offer (it's called the 'open market option'). A slightly more advantageous rate could make a difference of several hundred pounds a year to your income. If you're careful and do your homework well, you will do much better than if you just accept the first deal that's put on the table on your 65th birthday.

Note that there are certain personal characteristics – some under your control, some not – that will impact on the kind of annuity rate you are eligible for. One of these is your sex. Sad to say, women get a far worse deal on annuity rates than men because their life expectancy is higher. Since most women live longer, the insurance companies must plan on smaller annuity payments in order to stretch out the funds over a longer lifespan. (A sex change operation at the age of 64 probably won't make a difference to your annuity, though – and think of the cost of buying a whole new wardrobe!)

Your health status may also affect your annuity purchase. Ironically, smokers get better annuity rates than non-smokers, because the insurers don't expect smokers to live as long. The same applies to people with certain pre-existing medical conditions, such as cancer, heart disease and diabetes. (Of course, smokers and those with pre-existing conditions lose out in other ways. For example, they may find it hard to buy life insurance and they suffer from high medical costs as well as all the disadvantages that go with illness.)

In addition, when choosing an annuity, you will need to make a series of decisions concerning specific optional features – what could be called 'bells and whistles'. When comparing annuity deals, make sure you compare like with like. For instance, an inflation-linked joint-life annuity may not look good compared with a single-life level annuity, but it may be a better deal. Here is a list of the most important annuity features you'll need to consider.

- **Date of purchase.** Do you want to buy your annuity straight away or would you rather wait? Some retirees buy the annuity at age 65; others prefer to wait till age 70 or 75. If you wait, you give your investment pot longer to grow, but you are taking a risk that annuity rates might fall in the meantime (although you'll be that much older so will get a better annuity rate).
- **Income drawdown.** If you decide to wait a while, do you want to withdraw some income in the meantime? This is known as *income drawdown*, and there are limits to how much you can take from your pension pot. As a general rule, you are allowed to take out around the same amount per year as an annuity would have provided. Of course, when you do this, you are decreasing the size of your lump sum and therefore reducing the value of the annuity you will purchase later. Under the new A-Day pension rules established by the government, this system for drawing an income from your nest egg until you reach age 75 is known as an *unsecured pension*. Any trained financial adviser should be able to help you set up an unsecured pension that will suit your financial needs, but because of the added risk it is only suitable for people with large pension funds and for those prepared to take the risk.
- **Work continuation.** Are you phasing out your working life gradually, perhaps going part-time or taking on free-lance contracts? If so, you can opt for a phased retirement, using different portions of your pension fund to buy annuities at two or more stages up to the age of 75. This way you won't be relying on getting the best annuity rate at a particular moment around your 65th birthday. Instead, you can strike when the rates look good.

- **Investment linkage.** Would you like your retirement income to be linked to stock market performance or the growth of a with-profits fund? If so, consider an investment-linked annuity, which benefits from price rises in the market. Of course, any investment linked to the stock market may suffer losses as well, as it has done recently.
- **Payment schedule.** Do you want your annuity payments made monthly, quarterly or annually? Don't automatically choose monthly, but ask to see printouts illustrating each of the options. You will get a better deal with quarterly or annual payments made in arrears.
- **Inflation indexing.** A *level annuity* will pay you the same amount every year for the rest of your life. Inflation will decrease the buying power of that amount as you get older – a problem for most people, unless you believe that you won't need as much income in your mid-80s as in your mid-70s. If you want your income to remain the same in real terms (and particularly if you anticipate a lengthy retirement – if you are lucky enough to come from a long-lived family, for example), you should opt for an *inflation-linked annuity*. It will start with a (sometimes significantly) lower income than a level one of the same value, but will rise each year in line with prices. Over the long haul, the sum you'll receive will be roughly the same as with a level annuity, but the payment pattern will more closer mirror changes in prices.
- **Spousal income.** Do you want your partner to continue getting payments after your death? If so, you may want to purchase a *joint-life annuity* rather than a *single-life plan*. This can prove expensive, especially if your partner is younger than you, so before making a deal, compare this option with taking out a single-life annuity but buying a separate life insurance policy to provide a lump sum for your partner on your death. You may find that this

alternative is cheaper yet provides your partner with the same income protection.

- **Payment guarantee.** Some annuity policies offer guaranteed payments to your partner for up to ten years, even if you die the day after signing on the dotted line. Ten-year guarantees can be expensive, but some five-year guarantees don't cost any more than annuities without a guarantee at all.

As you can see, choosing an annuity can be a complex task. Start early, and take your time. There are big differences among kinds of annuities, and selecting one with the wrong combination of features for you can needlessly reduce your income by as much as 30 per cent. Many people enlist the help of a financial adviser when the time comes to buy an annuity. It's a good idea, especially if you work closely with your adviser (as I explained in chapter 6) to make sure you *really* understand all your options and end up with a choice that you will be comfortable with for the rest of your life.

How to Invest Your Nest Egg on Retirement

When your retirement date arrives, you will probably want to consider the purchase of an annuity, following the guidelines and suggestions I just offered. At the same time, you will be faced with choices as to how to invest any portion of your nest egg that does *not* go into an annuity.

This nest egg investment can take three forms:

- An *unsecured pension*, as described above. This is a temporary alternative to buying an annuity, which may last from the time you retire until age 75. An unsecured pension provides you with income drawdown based on the results obtained by your investments. When you turn 75, you will be required to secure a lifetime income, either by buying an annuity or converting your unsecured pension into an *alternatively secured pension.*

- An *alternatively secured pension* is a new option created by the A-Day pensions reform. If you choose this route, you will invest your retirement funds beginning at age 75 so as to generate a monthly income to support you.

- Finally, most people who have saved for a pension over the years will be entitled to a cash lump sum on retirement. This sum is over and above the money you may use to purchase an annuity. If you've invested in a money-purchase scheme, you can generally take 25 per cent of your entire retirement savings as a lump sum, as with most final salary schemes, depending on the scheme rules (occupational schemes don't have to let you take some money as tax-free cash). A word of warning. For those in final salary schemes, it might be very tempting to take 25 per cent as a lump sum. This could be a mistake because you may be giving up a very valuable final salary benefit. Make sure you get good advice on this decision.

Of course, you don't have to take that final 25 per cent as a lump-sum payment at all. Instead, you could leave it in the fund to buy a better annuity. For example, suppose you've built up a retirement fund of £600,000, you could use the entire £600,000 to buy an annuity. At current rates, you might receive an annual income of around £42,000.

Alternatively, you could take the 25 per cent cash lump sum of £150,000 and spend it – perhaps to buy a flat, pay off an existing mortgage or buy a second home. Then you could buy an annuity with the remaining £450,000, which might provide an annual income of around £31,500.

Or you could buy the £450,000 annuity (producing the income of £31,500), then invest the £150,000 in some other way to top up your income. Depending on the success of your investments, you might do better than you would have by spending the entire amount on an annuity.

In this case, you will have a sizeable amount of money that needs to be invested somehow on your retirement. (And the same would be true, of course, if you opt for either an unsecured pension or an alternatively secured pension.) Given your stage of life, and the fact that you will have stopped or reduced working, you will probably want to invest this money so as to enjoy 1) steady income, 2) relative safety and 3) at least modest long-term growth, in case you experience a lengthy retirement. What are the best investment choices for achieving these three objectives?

As with all investment planning, the decision is up to you. There's no one-size-fits-all solution, since each individual's financial status, health, lifestyle requirements and investor psychology is unique. It's definitely worthwhile getting financial advice as to how to invest it. There are a number of options you may want to consider.

One approach to retirement investing is *bond laddering*. This is a way of producing a predictable income for every year of your retirement. It involves investing an amount equal to a year's living expenses in high-quality bonds timed to mature in each year of your retirement.

You could start with five years' worth of bonds. Thus, if you estimate your annual living expenses at £30,000, you would invest that amount in one-year bonds; the same amount in two-year bonds; and the same amount in three-year, four-year and five-year bonds. You will have invested a total of £150,000, and your first five years of retirement life will be covered, since each year you will have access both to the interest income from your bonds as well as the principal from the bonds that are maturing that year.

Of course, you will also need to extend your bond ladder for further years as your retirement continues, using some of your interest income as well as money from other sources (such as shares or other investments that you gradually sell off). This is a system that requires professional advisory help to plan and execute successfully.

Another option is to manage your investment portfolio for maximum income, choosing shares that yield significant dividend income, relatively high-yielding bonds or unit trusts that invest in either of these kinds of securities. You can then plan to live mostly or entirely on the income generated by your investments, allowing the principal to continue to accumulate in your account. This means, of course, that your income may vary from year to year, depending on market conditions and the performance of your investments, and with it your lifestyle may need to be adjusted from year to year as well.

If you have gained some experience in share investing and feel comfortable with a portion of your funds in the stock market, consider the following system for setting up an after-retirement portfolio:

- Put half your money into well-run, low-risk unit trusts that invest in shares. An index-tracker fund, as described in chapter 5, may be a good choice. Reinvest any dividends you receive. This half of your portfolio should grow, slowly but steadily, throughout your retirement.
- Put the other half of your money into gilts, low-risk corporate bonds or unit trusts that invest in such bonds. This half of your portfolio should generate regular income payments.

With a bit of luck, and some careful budgeting, the kind of 50/50 portfolio I just described will allow you to withdraw funds to live on every month without making a huge dent in your capital. If you have a large enough nest egg, you should find that, ten or 20 years from now, the amount of money in your account is roughly the same as at the start of your retirement.

This plan is best for those who are comfortable with the idea of risk and will still sleep at night if they lose money. If you are highly risk-averse – and if you have a nest egg big enough to generate enough no-risk income to live on – consider keeping your lump sum money in a high-interest bank or building society account. Make sure you spread your money around so you're well protected by the bank compensation scheme. The Northern Rock crisis showed how quickly situations can change. Some banks share a banking licence (where they've taken over another bank or bought out a building society). It means you're only allowed a maximum of £50,000 compensation per licence, not per bank you're with.

Or look into the various National Savings and Investment products, including Guaranteed Income bonds. As I write, their income yields aren't spectacular but they are very secure.

Much the same can be said of the so-called guaranteed income bonds issued by life insurance companies. These allow you to choose to receive interest payments monthly or annually, or to select a growth option if you want to get back more than just your full capital. Finally, gilts – government bonds – are a very safe option, as are high-rated corporate bonds, those with AAA or AA ratings.

Whatever investment plan you choose for your retirement portfolio, continue to monitor your money over time. Keep track of all the investments you choose at least quarterly, and sell when you think you've got all the mileage you can out of a particular security. Keep moving from higher-risk towards lower-risk as you get older, and don't sell so much within a tax year that you incur capital gains tax liabilities. Instead, keep sales spread out to use your capital gains allowance each year; in 2009–10, this allowance is £10,100.

We're in the home stretch now – just a few more loose ends to take care of before we bid you a happy retirement. Read on . . .

9. After You've Retired

Life After Work: Managing Your Money

Congratulations! You've said goodbye to the hurly-burly of office politics, bought your annuities, invested your lump sum, and settled down for a rewarding life-after-work. Maybe you're now spending your days pottering in the garden, painting watercolours or playing with the grandchildren. Perhaps you've bought a speedboat and taken up waterskiing, gone back to university to study art history or archaeology, or taken a grand tour around the world. Or perhaps you've launched a new career as a school teacher, a volunteer caregiver, an artist or craftsperson or a tour guide. Whatever your new lifestyle is like, it doesn't mean you can wash your hands of the responsibility of personal financial management.

You are probably living on a fixed income now (with the exception of some fluctuation in your investment income), and the possibility of additional windfalls is remote, so if you run up debts it could be tricky to clear them. Set yourself a realistic monthly spending budget and work hard to stick to it. And as I've already suggested, keep close tabs on your investments and make adjustments to them as necessary.

If money's a bit tight, you might decide to sell some assets. With gold, silver, antiques, art and collectibles, you would be well advised to work through a reputable dealer. The additional value you'll realise this way should more than justify the 10 to 40 per cent commission you can expect to pay. Get quotes from at least three dealers before you hand over your property. Don't ever be tempted to pawn goods. It's just an extremely expensive way of borrowing money and you risk losing your valuables for much less than they're worth.

If you're strapped for cash and live in a mortgage-free property, you might be tempted to opt for an *equity-release scheme*. These arrangements give you cash in hand now and let the lender reclaim their money (and interest) from the sale of the property after your death. This will mean, of course, that you won't be able to pass the property on to your descendants. However, your immediate cash-flow problems will be solved and you'll still have a roof over your head.

Personally, I'm not keen on equity-release schemes because they tend to offer very unfavourable terms, but I recognise that you might find yourself in a position where you don't have much choice. Here are two ways the schemes can work:

Lifetime mortgages lend you a set amount, usually between 20 and 50 per cent of the property's value. You don't have to make any repayments while you're alive and you can continue living in the house while borrowing against its value. You are charged interest on the money you owe and the interest is added to the total debt, which can grow quickly. It might not be long before the lender is able to reclaim the entire value of your house after your death, even though you've only received a percentage of its value.

The advantage of a lifetime mortgage is that you can take money as a lump sum (or a series of lump sums) or a stream of monthly payments. Signing up for a lifetime mortgage can give you income and is therefore a tempting way to improve your retirement lifestyle if the value of your home has greatly increased in recent years. But there are serious pitfalls to be aware of. Your heirs may be forced to sell your home before they want to. And the interest charges and fees associated with a lifetime mortgage may be high – often higher than with a conventional mortgage.

Home reversion schemes buy all or a portion of your home for a sum that is much less than its market value. However, they let you live there for the rest of your life. Note that you are still responsible for the property's upkeep even though it is no longer legally 'yours'.

If you want to take out a home reversion plan or lifetime mortgage, make sure that the company has a policy of not taking away your home before you die and capping the amount you owe to the value of the property. Rather than opt for either of these equity-release schemes, my advice would be, if possible, to sell the house yourself for a fair market price and either buy somewhere cheaper or move into a rental home. However, I understand that you may not want to move from the family home you've lived in for decades.

Alternatively, if your kids are keen to inherit the property one day, why not ask them to subsidise you in the meantime to protect their inheritance? Explain to them that otherwise you will be forced to join the SKI Club (SKI = Spend the Kids' Inheritance).

Another reason to avoid equity-release schemes is because you will have lost your last area of financial flexibility. It could become very tricky if you want to move at a later date, or need some cash to pay for long-term care. Leave such schemes for the last resort.

Living Arrangements as You Age

Up to this point, we've been focusing on planning for an active, healthy retirement in which you will live independently and get a chance to enjoy some of the leisure activities you haven't had time to participate in while working.

Happily, this is what retirement is like for most people. But statistics show that one man in six and one woman in four will need long-term care at some point in life. For many people, the need arises not in 'early retirement' (between ages 65 and 75), but in 'advanced retirement' (after age 75). This is when you may find that your changing physical and mental condition makes it difficult or impossible to live alone and take care of your own needs. And while this doesn't mean that your life can't still be rich and enjoyable, it does have an impact on your lifestyle and your financial status.

The first issue to consider in regard to long-term care is deciding whether or not you actually need it. If you're uncertain as to whether or not you should continue to live at home, consider contacting your local social services or community care department to ask for a *needs assessment* (otherwise known as a *'care assessment'*). This is a free service to which you're entitled, regardless of your financial situation. A social worker will visit you to ask about how you're coping at home and to discuss your plans and wishes for the future.

The goal is not to shunt people into nursing homes but rather to help them live as independently as possible. So if you're able to live on your own with just a bit of outside help – for example, with some assistance in dealing with housework, shopping or preparing meals – the social worker will try to arrange this support. Known as *home care* or *domiciliary care,* this kind of help may be provided on a 24-hour basis (if needed, such as in the aftermath of an accident or illness) or for just a few hours a week. Depending on your financial situation, you may have to pay.

On the other hand, if your physical and mental condition is such that you need more assistance than this, the social worker may be able to advise you on further options. If not, contact the independent advice charity the Elderly Accommodation Counsel (EAC) at www.eac.org.uk. These options may include:

- A *retirement home* or *assisted living home,* in which residents live in their own homes within a special facility set aside for elder care. For example, they may live in a separate cottage in which they can cook meals and otherwise care for themselves, while sharing such facilities as lounges and recreational areas and, when needed, having access to help with activities like shopping, laundry or housework.
- A *residential care home,* in which residents can receive help with such daily tasks as bathing, dressing and eating, as well as help with simple medical procedures (such as administration of medicines) as needed. Some elderly people live in a residential care home on a long-term basis (for years or decades), while others stay just for a few months, for instance while recovering from surgery or illness.
- A *nursing home,* in which nursing and other medical care is regularly provided in addition to the kinds of support offered in a residential care home. A nursing home is staffed with registered nurses and experienced care assistants who can offer services prescribed by a physician, including physiotherapy and cancer care.

In addition to the needs assessment, you are also entitled to a *financial assessment*, which will determine whether or not your local council will pay for some or all of your future care.

On average, residential care costs around £24,000 per year. If nursing care is required, this will increase the costs by another £5,000 or so. Depending on your assets – the amount you have in savings, investments and property – your local council may not take them into account when assessing your contribution to care costs. The National Health Service will pay only for the nursing care you receive, if any (the system is different in Scotland).

While you are living in a care home, you are entitled to a number of government benefits, including:

- Attendance allowance: a tax-free payment for people over the age of 65 who have health problems or physical or mental disabilities.
- Disability living allowance: provides payment for those *under* 65 who cannot live without care or have difficulties getting around.
- Pension credit: paid to those over the age of 60 with limited incomes.
- Savings credit: an additional pension credit for those over 65 with limited savings.
- Council tax benefit: helps those on low income pay council tax bills.

However, note that some of these benefits are means-tested: they are available only to those with very limited income and assets, including property. If you must move into a long-term care facility and don't have sufficient income to pay for your care, you may find that the local authorities will, in effect, force you to sell your home to pay for the cost of care if you live on your own (but not if your spouse still lives there).

Perhaps it will occur to you that if you give away your assets you may be entitled to support from your local council that you otherwise wouldn't receive. With this in mind, some people try to sign over ownership of their homes and their investments to their children just before going into a care home, believing this will entitle them to free support. Unfortunately, this probably won't work. The local council is supposed to investigate cases where assets were given away or transferred as a way of claiming government benefits (the ploy is called *deprivation of assets*), and they have the right to decide to treat these assets as if you still own them.

Of course, the timing is key: if you give away your assets one month before entering a nursing home, you will surely arouse suspicion. If you gave them away ten years earlier, you probably won't.

I urge you to play fair – don't try to manipulate the system to gain benefits to which you're not entitled. But by the same token, don't cheat yourself out of benefits you deserve (and which your lifelong tax payments have helped to make possible) through carelessness or inertia.

In recent years, journalistic investigations and court cases (such as the now famous Coughlan case of 1999) have revealed that some elderly or disabled people have been unfairly denied funding by local councils that were strapped for cash and looking for opportunities to cut costs.

If you feel you've been denied benefits unjustly, or if the criteria on which your request for benefits has been denied appear to be inconsistent or confusing, you have the right to question the decision. Complain to the local authorities, contact advice charities such as Citizens Advice or Age Concern and Help the Aged (called AgeUK from 2010), or your local MP and enlist the advice of a solicitor if you're not satisfied with the answers you receive.

Paying for Long-Term Care

As you see, long-term care can be complex and expensive. And depending on your financial situation, the government may or may not provide help with the bills. Furthermore, a government-paid long-term care arrangement may not necessarily rise to the standard you'd like. Care homes vary in quality, and most observers agree that the nicest are generally those with a preponderance of private (self-paid) residents rather than those sponsored by the government.

You'll also find that, if you have private medical insurance, it will generally not cover the costs of long-term care. Such insurance is designed to defray expenses associated with acute, short-term conditions – illnesses or accidents from which recovery is normally expected. Long-term care required because of conditions of ageing, ranging from arthritis to Alzheimer's disease, is not included.

So what can you do to ensure that you will receive the kind of long-term care you want and need? Some older people end up relying on help from their children, but you'd probably prefer to avoid this possibility since it burdens your family members and may lead to tension and unhappiness. There are a number of better strategies to consider:

- One possibility is to sell your home *before* you need long-term care and move into a smaller, less expensive place or a room in a relative's home. The money thus freed up can be invested as a fund for eventual use in paying for long-term care.
- Another option is to remain in your home and free up some of the equity through an equity-release scheme or lifetime mortgage, as discussed earlier. Again, the money this makes available can be invested to create a long-term care fund.
- A third option is to buy an insurance policy designed to defray the costs of long-term care.

Let's take a closer look at this third option, since there are several kinds of long-term insurance policies you may want to consider.

One type of policy is the *immediate care plan*. This is a type of annuity that you buy when you have already been medically assessed as needing care. Like other annuities, it provides a guaranteed lifetime income in return for a lump sum investment. The cost of the policy depends, in part, on your health status; a person who is expected to live longer will pay somewhat more for the same level of monthly income. As with other annuities, you can buy an immediate care plan that is indexed to rise with inflation, or choose one with level payments that do not increase over time. Some immediate care plans make payments directly to the care home, while others pay the insured person.

A second type of policy is the *deferred care plan*. This is a variation on the immediate care plan which also makes annuity payments for life in return for a lump sum investment. As with an immediate care plan, you buy the deferred care plan when you know you need long-term care. However, the payments don't begin until a specified number of months or years have passed. This is a good option if, for example, you have savings that will pay for five years' worth of care but are concerned about expenses beyond that period. Since your investment will have time to grow during the deferral period, a deferred care plan will generally save you a lot of money as compared with an immediate care plan.

A third option is the *pre-funded care plan*. This is an insurance policy you buy before you need long-term care, and, in fact, before you know whether or not you will need such care at all. Most people who purchase such a policy wait until they are at least in their 50s, after they have begun thinking about the possibility of needing long-term care but while they are still fit and healthy.

The provisions of pre-funded care plans vary quite a bit. Some are paid for by a lump sum investment, others through monthly premiums. Some will pay you for life after the need for long-term care arises; others have a time limit of a fixed number of years. Some offer level payments, others payments that are indexed to rise with inflation. And some will pay a death benefit if you die without needing care, while others do not. Each of these variations will affect the cost of the plan and the benefits you can expect to receive.

If you're considering buying a pre-funded care plan, look carefully at the exclusions. Many policies will *not* pay out if care is required due to dependence on alcohol or illegal drugs, attempted suicide, depression or other mental illnesses, or HIV/AIDS.

In addition, bear in mind the realistic odds on the 'bet' you are making. As I noted earlier, up to one person in four will need long-term care at some point in life. But that means that three people in four will *not* need such care. So if you are an 'average' person, the odds are good that an investment in a pre-funded care plan will *not* provide you with any financial return. This doesn't necessarily mean that buying such a policy is a bad idea. It does mean that you should think carefully before making this kind of investment, and don't use funds that you really need for other, more pressing needs.

Passing Your Wealth Along

If people tend to neglect their pensions because they can't bear to think about getting old, they are even worse when it comes to writing a will. It's almost as if they fear that acknowledging the reality of death will hasten the dreaded day. At least half of all adults in the UK have not yet made a will, and many never do. They die *intestate*. In most cases, this will mean that their possessions don't go to the beneficiaries they would have chosen. It's crazy not to spend a little time and money making up a document that will mean your wishes are carried out after your death and your family are looked after, rather than forcing them to squabble in court.

Here are the basic things you need to think about when planning your estate.

- **Do it yourself or get legal help.** You can buy a DIY will form from a stationery office, use a specialist wills company or hire a solicitor. A DIY form may be all right if your affairs are *extremely* simple or if you want to leave everything to a single heir. However, for the vast majority of people, I recommend working with a solicitor who specialises in wills. He or she will anticipate many complications and options that the average person would never consider. Your solicitor may also give you advice about how best to structure your will to have the end result you want. If you wish, they can also act as your *executor* (that is, the person who will implement your will after you die). And of course, a solicitor will make sure your will is legally binding. If you're concerned about costs, think carefully about how you want to handle your estate before your first meeting with the solicitor. This will save you time and make the will-writing process simpler and more effective.

- **Plan your bequests.** Decide who should get what, and name the person who gets whatever is left after all specified assets have been distributed. This list should include your main bequests plus any special gifts – 'My model train collection to my nephew Harry', for example. When specifying monetary bequests, think in terms of percentages rather than pound figures, since the latter will change over time as investments and savings fluctuate.

- **Choose an executor.** He or she is responsible for making sure all your wishes are carried out. A family member or a trusted friend would be suitable, so long as he or she is reasonably intelligent and trustworthy (but consult them first). Using your bank or solicitor is an obvious option, but it can be expensive. Also select a second executor who will step in if your first executor dies before you or at the same time (as in a car crash that kills two family members).

- **Provide for your children.** If you have children under the age of 18, your will should state who should look after them in the event of your demise. (Again, this naturally requires advance consultation and planning.) If you have specific desires for their education or living arrangements, you may want to mention those here. You will also need to nominate a trustee to manage any money you are leaving for the care of the children until they reach adulthood. This could be a trusted banker, solicitor, family member or other adviser. Finally, you may also choose to nominate an animal-loving guardian for any pets you might leave behind.

- **Offer any special instructions.** What do you want to happen to your body – cremation, burial, donation to a medical school? Are there plans you want to leave behind for a family business? Are there distant relatives or old friends you want your executor to contact after you pass away? It's useful to write down instructions like these and store them along with your will so they won't be overlooked at a time of emotional distress.
- **Store your will carefully.** Get two signatories to witness your will, and then keep it in a safe place. Make sure your executors know where it is so they're not turning the house upside down after your funeral. Better still, give them each a copy.

Review your will if any major life circumstances change – for example, if you get married, have children or if the people you've named as heirs die before you. Note that previous wills become invalid if you marry after making them (except in Scotland). You can always make revisions to former wills, but if you decide to write a new one, be sure to start it by saying that it revokes all previous ones, otherwise things could get very confusing. Again, your solicitor can make sure that all these details are properly in place.

If you have a significant estate, you may be concerned about inheritance tax. The inheritance tax threshold is currently £325,000 (2009–10) or £650,000 for a married couple or those in a civil partnership. Pensions and life insurance policies on top of the value of a family home can easily take you over this limit, in which case your loved ones will have to pay tax after your death. To avoid this, you should take advice from an independent financial adviser or solicitor specialising in inheritance tax. There may be measures you can take to reduce the amount of inheritance tax you pay while enabling your beneficiaries to get easier access to some of your estate. If it is outside your estate for tax purposes, your beneficiaries do not have to wait until probate has been granted to access it.

Another way of avoiding inheritance tax is by making financial gifts to relatives prior to your passing. However, this can be a tricky strategy. The gifts are, of course, irrevocable, which means you must plan carefully so as not to find yourself caught short of money you need for your own support. There are also legal limitations as to the amounts you can give. The government doesn't want people in their final weeks of life making massive last-minute gifts simply as a way of evading inheritance tax.

If you have a large estate and are interested in exploring ways to minimise your after-death tax burden, consult a financial adviser and a solicitor to discuss the latest regulations and to devise a plan that makes sense for you.

Your family will be grateful.

Epilogue:
Money for Life

When my dear friend Roger retired, the first thing he did was something you could probably never guess: he left for a ten-day holiday in Guatemala. It was his first trip to that lush and fascinating but little-visited Central American country.

What was behind this choice? 'I wanted something *interesting* to talk about,' Roger told me later, with a laugh. 'I've known too many retired people who can only discuss their golf game and their latest ailments.' Instead, Roger came home with colourful photos, tales of adventure in the jungle, and recipes for exotic dishes he'd never tasted before. Most of his conversations now end with people saying, 'You must really be enjoying your retirement' – often with a trace of envy in their voices.

Money, as you've seen in the pages of this book, is one important key to making a smooth transition into a happy retirement. Smart financial planning brings with it a sense of comfort and security. But even more important is knowing yourself and what you want out of retirement.

For some people, the joy of retirement can come simply from the freedom to do what you want: to spend the day reading a book, playing a game of tennis, working in the garden, visiting an art gallery with a friend, or doing nothing at all. It can come from the freedom to take that long-dreamed-of holiday without having to worry about what's happening at the office or counting the days till you're due back at work.

For other people, retirement is all about being open to new

possibilities. Perhaps you'll decide to take the skills and knowledge you've developed at work and apply them in a different industry. Or perhaps you'll want to try turning a much-loved hobby into a money-making vocation, or go back to college to learn a new occupation. Some retirees end up creating a second career that is more creative, enjoyable and rewarding than the first.

And for other people, the greatest joy of retirement lies in the opportunity to give something back to their local community or to the world at large. Volunteering or getting involved in some socially conscious activity can bring an exciting sense of purpose and fulfilment to your retirement. Lillian Carter, mother of the former US president Jimmy Carter, joined the Peace Corps and worked in Africa after her retirement. Her inspiring book about this experience, *Letters Home*, shows how this experience revitalised her.

Miss Lillian's son Jimmy followed in her footsteps. After leaving the White House, he and his wife Rosalynn embarked on a second career of global peacemaking, charitable work and book authorship – and in their 70s they learned how to ski.

Of course, you needn't be a world figure like Jimmy Carter to donate your time and talents. You can tackle a reduced-pay or no-pay position, depending on your circumstances, at an organisation whose goals you support. You can work as a volunteer at a local school, hospital, shelter or arts organisation. You can become involved in social activism or local politics. All of these are ways to pass on some of your hard-earned wisdom to the world, as well as to express your gratitude for the blessings of life.

If your finances are in proper order, you'll be prepared to pursue a life in retirement that is on your own terms, freed from the daily demands of work. But what are 'your own terms'? Have you thought about them *before* retiring? It's a question people need to begin considering in their 40s and 50s – especially in today's uncertain world, where involuntary retirement may strike at almost any time.

I recently spoke with a friend in his late 50s who admitted (much to his own surprise, I suspect) that he had no plans for retirement. 'I guess I'll continue plodding along until I'm 65, when I'll *have* to retire,' Donald told me. 'Then I'll figure something out.'

I took a deep breath, then said, 'Donald, I truly hate to tell you this. But you are making a big mistake. You need to start thinking about retirement *now* – not after the farewell party. People who put off planning for their lives after work usually end up frustrated, confused, even depressed. I know – I've seen it happen too many times.'

After all, a happy retirement is not an entitlement. Paradoxically, it's something you need to work at – at least a little.

Fortunately, you and I don't need to start from scratch when it comes to devising a smart retirement programme. Many people have travelled this path before us. After speaking with many retired friends, relatives and acquaintances, I compiled the following two lists: one containing five things to do when you retire, and another with five things to avoid. These ideas will help ensure that your years of retirement are a time of increasing fun, pleasure and growth – not one of stagnation, boredom and decline.

Your Retirement To-Do List

- *Stay physically and mentally active*. Don't become the kind of retired person who says, 'I'm looking for things to help fill up the day.' Retirement shouldn't be a wasteland of time to be killed. Instead, get out of the house and take up activities that will force you to move your body and your mind in new and interesting ways. Try a new hobby, an art form or a sport (with advice from your doctor, of course). Take up dancing, swimming, gardening or walking. Sign up for classes at the local college or art museum; learn a new skill, like furniture-making or embroidery; tackle the books you've always meant to read, the classic movies you've never seen, or the great music you've never heard. Or write a book of your own – your life story, perhaps – which your children and grandchildren will find fascinating, even if no one else does!

- *Plan retired life with your partner.* A sad stereotype of retirement is the spouse with suddenly nothing to do, who finds himself (or herself) a stranger in their own home. The wife of one newly-retired friend of mine became so exasperated she told him, 'Don't you have anything to do? I'm so tired of seeing the back of your head!' Another person who retired from his job as a factory efficiency expert decided to spend his time showing his wife how she could handle the household chores more efficiently. (His advice didn't go down very well). Retirement can be a strain on any marriage or partnership. Talk through what you plan to do in retirement and discuss the adjustments you may each have to make. Don't assume you must spend every hour together. In fact, it can be very helpful to plan some time apart every day – shopping, visiting friends, taking classes or just going for a walk. Even the most loving relationship can get irritating when it becomes overly familiar.

- *Set goals to look forward to.* I think of a friend's parents who are in their 80s, having retired almost 20 years ago. They are always planning their next trip. Every time I meet them it's fascinating because they enjoy talking about what they learned from their last trip and what they're looking forward to from their next. Their retirement years are focused on the new adventures they are creating for themselves and sharing with their children and grandchildren, who marvel at them. It keeps them interested and interesting – important aspects of a satisfying retirement. You can do the same, even if travel is beyond your means or simply not your cup of tea. Learn to play an instrument – and set the goal of becoming proficient enough to join a local musical group within a year. Try writing your first short story or poem – and be brave enough to read it aloud at the 'open mike' night at the local writers' club. Become a volunteer fund-raiser for a local charity – and aim to raise a record amount for their coffers during the next year. Give yourself something enjoyable and stimulating to wake up for every morning as well as something to think about with pleasure when you go to bed every night.

- *Think long and hard before pulling up stakes.* For some people, a happy retirement includes moving to a new home – perhaps a smaller place that demands less work to maintain, or a house or flat in a warmer climate. But don't rush into a retirement move. Many retirees who move in haste find that the dislocation they suffer leaves them lonely and unhappy. Think about the family, friends and surroundings you will leave behind; the familiar physicians, shopkeepers, clergy and others whose services you may miss; the comfortable routines that will be disrupted. Thoroughly research the place you are considering moving to and spend as much extended time there as possible before making any irrevocable decisions.
- *Keep up your old friendships and make some new ones.* For many people, leaving work means leaving behind a major social outlet. It's often difficult to maintain friendships with people who are no longer your

colleagues; the retiree becomes an 'outsider' who is no longer part of the inside game of work. So it's important to work extra hard at maintaining non-work-related friendships and starting new ones. If you find it hard to meet people, join clubs, classes, volunteer groups or a local house of worship. If you spend time and get involved in activities you enjoy, you'll find yourself chatting with people who share your interests. Soon you'll be part of a new circle of friends.

Your Retirement To-Avoid List

- *Avoid getting trapped in someone else's stereotype.* Don't conform to a 'retired person' stereotype that others – your family or children, your employer or even the government – may try to impose on you. After all your years on this earth, you should know yourself well. Live the way *you* want to live, whether other people approve or not.
- *Avoid becoming a know-it-all or a stick-in-the-mud.* As we get older, it's easy to fall into the trap of thinking and talking too much about 'the good old days', 'the way we used to do it' and 'when I was young'. Don't misunderstand me – the memories you have of the good times in your life and the wisdom you've gleaned from experience are both very valuable and worth sharing. But when every third remark from your lips looks back 20 years or more, it's a sign that you've stopped looking forward – which means you are probably becoming a bore both to those around you and to yourself. Immerse yourself in the life of *today* and you'll find that the 'old times' are no longer quite so compelling a topic of discussion.
- *Avoid letting inertia control your life.* For some people, once work disappears as a motivating force, it's hard to

stay active. They find themselves waking up later and later each day; they stay in their pyjamas or nightgowns till nine, then till ten and eventually all day long; they leave the house only when the refrigerator is bare; and the television ends up being on 24 hours a day, their sole companion and source of stimulation. Don't let this happen to you. Schedule activities that will force you to get up, get dressed and get out. You'll enjoy your retirement far more if you're not *too* retired.

- *Avoid neglecting your finances.* If you've done a good job of planning for retirement, congratulations! Now continue to monitor your savings and investments as the years pass. Check on the growth of your money at least once a month; keep the records of your current account up-to-date; and monitor any unusual changes in your retirement funds.

- *Avoid being too proud to ask for help.* Many people who have been self-sufficient all their lives feel embarrassed or ashamed to find that, in retirement, they sometimes need help with things. You shouldn't. Remember the times you helped a parent, relative, neighbour or friend (and were probably glad to do it), and don't feel awkward about seeking help when you need it. It may involve physical chores that are a bit too hard for you to manage; it may involve some financial or administrative task you find complex or hard to understand. (And you don't need to be elderly to find computer software, tax rules or bank policies confusing!) Call on those around you for assistance; the chances are good they will be happy to help.

Yes, finances are important when it comes to planning your retirement. But there's one thing that's even more precious and more irreplaceable than money – and that's time. Figuring out what you want to do with your time and how you can make it as enjoyable and rewarding as possible is the single most important thing you can do to guarantee that the final decades of your life are among the very best.

Index